IN THE KNOW IN

Japan

LIVING LANGUAGE®

TERRA COGNITA™

Also available from

Business Companion: Japanese

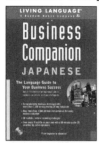

A perfect complement to *In the Know in Japan*—this is an essential language guide for working with Japanese colleagues. The 416-page handbook contains more than 1,000 phrases for general business situations and vocabulary for over 25 specific industries, plus a two-way glossary, measurements, useful addresses, Web sites, and more. The audio CD contains more than 500 phrases used in realistic, current business dialogues.

Handbook/CD program 1-4000-2042-5 $21.95/C$32.95
Handbook only 1-4000-2044-1 $12.95/C$19.95

Japanese Complete Course
For beginners or those who want a thorough review

The best-selling program that will have you speaking Japanese in just six weeks! Developed by U.S. government experts, it features a proven speed-learning method that progresses from words to phrases to complete sentences and dialogues. Includes a coursebook, a dictionary, and 40 lessons on two 90-minute cassettes or three 60-minute CDs.

Cassette program 1-4000-2018-2 $25.00/C$38.00 • CD program 1-4000-2019-0 $25.00/C$38.00 • Coursebook only 1-4000-2020-4 $8.00/C$12.00
Dictionary only 1-4000-2021-2 $5.95/C$8.95

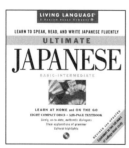

Ultimate Japanese: Basic-Intermediate

This comprehensive program is equivalent to two years of college-level study. Up-to-date conversations and vocabulary in each lesson teach reading, writing, grammar, and culture tips along with conversational skills. Includes a coursebook and more than 40 lessons on eight 60-minute cassettes or CDs. An advanced course is also available.

Cassette program 0-609-60762-6 $75.00/C$115.00 • CD program 0-609-60736-7 $75.00/C$115.00 • Coursebook only 0-609-80682-3 $18.00/C$27.50

Available at bookstores everywhere.
www.livinglanguage.com

300 West 49th Street Suite 314 New York, New York 10019 USA
Phone: 212.663.9890 Fax: 212.663.2404
E-mail: info@terracognita.com
www.terracognita.com

Know Your World

Terra Cognita provides top quality cross-cultural training service and re-sources. The goal of our cross-cultural learning material is to help you build the awareness and skills to recognize and respect cultural differ-ences you will encounter. Terra Cognita programs thereby ensure a sucessful adjustment to life in a new culture for expatriates and the skills necessary to succeed in international business.

Terra Cognita delivers cross-cultural learning with private seminars and workshops, with online learning modules, and with a variety of video, audio and printed material. Currently Terra Cognita programs meet the needs of expatriates and international business colleagues at various multinational companies, government agencies and educational institu-tions worldwide.

LIVE ABROAD! is an innovative video-based expatriate preparation program that covers the entire expatriate experience from preparing to go through the cul-tural adjustment process to the final return home.

WORK ABROAD! is a video-based program that ex-plains and vividly recreates the cross-cultural dy-namics of the international business environment.

For more information on Terra Cognita
and a wealth of articles and resources for cross-cultural learning,
visit our Web site at WWW.TERRACOGNITA.COM

V I D E O S   S E M I N A R S   O N L I N E

LIVING LANGUAGE®
A Random House Company

IN THE KNOW IN

Japan

THE INDISPENSABLE CROSS-CULTURAL GUIDE TO WORKING AND LIVING IN JAPAN

WRITTEN BY
Jennifer Phillips

EDITED BY
Suzanne McQuade

*Picked up 2nd fle floc
at Creanette*

Published in the United States by Living Language, A Random House Company

www.livinglanguage.com

Editor: Suzanne McQuade
Production Editor: Marina Padakis
Production Manager: Pat Ehresmann
Design: Barbara M. Bachman
Illustrations: Adrian Hashimi

Although all factual information in this book, such as Web sites, telephone numbers, etc., is as up-to-date as possible at press time, changes occur all the time, and Living Language cannot accept responsibility for the accuracy of the facts in the book or for inadvertent errors or omissions.

First Edition

ISBN 0-609-61114-3

Library of Congress Cataloging-in-Publication Data available upon request.

PRINTED IN THE UNITED STATES OF AMERICA

10 9 8 7 6 5 4 3 2 1

ACKNOWLEDGMENTS

Thanks to the many people who generously shared their experiences and ideas to make this book come together. A special thanks to my editor, Suzanne McQuade, for her expert guidance and patience.

And thanks to the rest of the Living Language team: Lisa Alpert, Elizabeth Bennett, Chris Warnasch, Zviezdana Verzich, Helen Tang, Pat Ehresmann, Denise De Gennaro, Linda Schmidt, Marina Padakis, Sophie Chin, Barbara Bachman, and Fuhito Shimoyama.

CONTENTS

Whether you're moving to Japan or traveling there for business, it's essential that you know what to expect, and what will be expected of you. Cross-cultural awareness provides you with just that knowledge. *In the Know in Japan* is designed to help both business people and their families navigate the often-complex waters of life in another culture. By culture we don't mean haiku poetry or Kabuki theater. Culture is the backdrop of every activity in which you engage in and every word you exchange. In Japan, you'll be dealing with a foreign culture every time you shake a colleague's hand, sit down to write an e-mail, get on a train, or even buy a loaf of bread. A list of "dos & don'ts" provides only part of the picture. A more thorough understanding of culture—what really motivates people's behaviors, attitudes, beliefs, and habits—will allow you, and any family members with you, to adapt with ease to both the social and business environments of Japan.

This book was developed to be easy, practical, and comprehensive. You'll first get your bearings through some general background information about Japan, such as its history, geography, political system, and social structure. This is no history text, though. The Background chapter is meant to be a brief survey that will familiarize you with some important landmarks you'll no doubt hear about or see. If something strikes you as interesting, the Background chapter will also serve you well as a way to get your feet wet in a particular area; we leave any further exploration of Japanese history up to you.

Next, you'll read an overview of Japanese culture. For our purposes, we've broken culture down into the following six categories: Time, Communication, Group Dynamics, Status and Hierarchy, Relationships, and Reasoning. This provides not only a general picture of the components of Japanese culture, but a very practical picture, too. However, while using these generalizations, we should never forget that any culture is made up of individuals, and individuals vary. Learning about these important general concepts, though, where differences and pitfalls abound, will better prepare you and your family for a more successful experience abroad.

The next chapter, Living Abroad, will give you some insight to the issues that people face in other cultures. You'll learn what to expect as a businessperson, a family member, a parent, a child, a single person, or a teenager. This chapter offers invaluable advice that applies to life in any other culture. It will raise the kinds of important questions you'll want to consider when preparing to make an adjustment to life abroad. Most importantly, it will prepare you to face some tough challenges, and then reap some wonderful benefits.

The next two chapters of the book, Getting Around and Living and Staying in Japan, are step-by-step guides to everyday life in Japan. They address the issues that everyone must deal with, from driving to taking buses, to shopping, to waiting in line, to social etiquette. These chapters are full of clearly organized information, practical lists, and essential tips. Everyone—single traveler, parent, or child—will benefit.

Next are two chapters designed specifically for the businessperson. In Business Environment, you'll get an idea of the general principles that govern working in Japan, from company values and structure, to chain of command, unions, workspace, and women in business. In the next chapter, Business Step-by-Step, you'll learn the essentials of doing business in Japan including dress, speeches and presentations, negotiations, and often overlooked but crucial details such as business card etiquette and making appointments.

Finally, we leave you with an introduction to the essentials of the Japanese language. While it is true that English is usually the lingua franca of global business, it cannot be denied that even a vary basic knowledge of a foreign language can make a world of difference. This is no full-service language course; you won't be memorizing any irregular verbs or grammar rules. But you'll find that the minimal amount of time it takes to learn some basic social expressions and survival vocabulary will be recouped a hundred times over. Your Japanese colleagues and friends will be very appreciative that you've made an effort to learn just a little of their language. You'll find that the experience of another language is often its own reward, and you may even want to go further and learn to speak Japanese more fluently.

Good luck, and enjoy. We hope you find this course informative, practical, and enriching.

ONE

BACKGROUND

Japan stands at the forefront of industrialized nations, both in Asia and worldwide. Following the devastation of World War II, Japan rebuilt itself into a thriving economic force, leading the way in the field of technology.

Japan is an enigma to many Westerners. Not only are the sights, sounds, and smells all different, but those invisible parts of culture, such as values and beliefs, are unfamiliar as well. If you will be journeying to Japan, either on a business visit or as an expatriate, you can help ensure a successful trip or transition by learning more about the country known as the Land of the Rising Sun.

VITAL STATISTICS

The following information is based on the latest available data at the time of writing.

Official Name:	Japan
Capital:	Tokyo
Federal Flag:	White background with red circle (symbolizing the sun) in the center
Area:	145,883 sq mi (377,835 sq km)
Land Distribution:	11% arable land, 1% permanent crops, 2% permanent pastures, 67% forests and woodland, 19% other
Highest Point:	Fujiyama (3,776 m)
Lowest Point:	Hachiro-gata (-4m)
Natural Resources:	Fish, trace amounts of minerals
Population (2001 est.):	126,771,662
Average Family Size:	2.8
Largest Cities:	Tokyo, Osaka, Kanagawa
Ethnicity:	99.4% Japanese; 0.6% other
Language:	Japanese
Literacy:	99%
Religions:	84% Buddhist and Shinto, 16% agnostic or other
Currency:	Japanese Yen

GNP (1999):	$4.7 trillion
GDP (1999):	$4.6 trillion
Major Trading Partners:	U.S., China, South Korea, Taiwan
Per Capita Income (1999):	$27,252
Inflation (2000):	-0.7%
Unemployment (2000):	4.7%
Employment by Industry:	65% services, 30% industry, 5% agriculture

GEOGRAPHY AND CLIMATE

Japan is an island nation that stretches in an arc covering some 3,000 kilometers. More than 80% of Japan's land mass is mountainous, much of it volcanic. Japan has four major islands—Honshū, Hokkaidō, Kyūshū, and Shikoku—and more than 1,000 smaller islands. With so many people packed into such a small area, it is inevitable that there are few uninhabited places left in Japan. Only the most inaccessible mountain peaks have avoided the stamp of humankind.

With more than 40 active volcanic mountains, Japan is one of the most seismically active countries in the world. Because of this, Japan has an abundance of hot springs. Along with this pleasure, however, comes frequent seismic activity throughout the island and the resultant earthquakes, volcanic eruptions, and tsunami (tidal waves).

The length of Japan's arc of islands means that there are significant climactic differences from one end to the other. The southern islands, such as Okinawa, have subtropical climates while the northern islands, such as Hokkaidō, see long winters with heavy snowfall and relatively brief summers. Weather patterns along the arc are also influenced by its proximity to the Asian continent. The western side of the arc, facing the Sea of Japan, is at the mercy of cold air masses moving down from Siberia during the winter, which meet the warmer, moist air moving from the Pacific, resulting in heavy snowfall. The eastern side of the arc, which abuts the Pacific Ocean, sees little snowfall, but the northern islands often experience very cold winters.

Summers in Japan are generally hot and, with the exception of some northern islands, humid. The rainy season generally starts in mid-May and lasts a few weeks. At the end of the summer, there is often a second period of heavy rainfall, frequently accompanied by typhoons and strong winds.

PEOPLE

Japan has a largely homogenous population; more than 99% of the population is ethnic Japanese. The largest group of non-Japanese, numbering fewer than 700,000, is the *zai-nichi kankoku-jin*, who are ethnically Korean. Most, however, were born in Japan and speak only Japanese. Other non-Japanese populations are generally foreign workers from many countries living temporarily in Japan.

The Ainu are the indigenous people of Hokkaidō. Anthropologists believe that the Ainu are a Caucasian race whose immigration patterns brought them to Japan from Siberia. Intermarriage with the Japanese has virtually eliminated the physical differences between the two races. Estimates place the Ainu population between 20,000 and 80,000, with only a few hundred pure-blooded Ainu remaining. The Ainu language is still used, although it has been almost totally replaced by Japanese. Ainu customs and traditions, which are animistic in nature, were outlawed for many decades and it was only in 1997 that the government mandated the promotion of the Ainu culture.

IMPORTANT ISSUES

Every nation has its share of problems, and Japan is no different. The Japanese are addressing a wide range of questions, from the viability of the education system to concerns about the influence of the U.S. and other Western countries on the Japanese culture. An aging population and a housing shortage are two of the major issues facing Japan in the short term. Of course, they are just a sampling of the many issues that are important to Japan and the Japanese.

Aging Population

With Japan's low birthrate and increased life spans, Japan's population is rapidly aging. It is predicted that within a few decades, more than 25% of the population will be over 65. This has several implications, the most obvious of which is that more services and government programs will be needed to support the aging population. The low birth rate means that a considerable burden will be placed on people of working age to pay for these programs.

Japan's economy will also be impacted as the face of the Japanese people ages. Seniors will become a major political force, ensuring that pension and health care programs continue to meet their needs. In addition, concerns loom about how the work force will be affected as more and more workers retire. In the current downturned economy, the loss of workers to retirement is positive, but this will not be the case during times of economic growth. Japan is already investing heavily in alternatives such as robotics to combat this potential problem.

Housing

Japan has a large population for a relatively small land area. Furthermore, about 75% of the population is packed into a few urban areas. This has led to overcrowded and overused roads, trains, and other infrastructure, but perhaps the most severe problem has been a shortage of housing. Apartments have become smaller and apartment buildings have grown taller in an effort to combat the problem, but space is still at a premium and affordable housing and home ownership is increasingly difficult.

Some people are quick to point out, too, that there are further, indirect issues that are impacted by the housing trends. The most important is the erosion of the family unit in Japan. Long gone are the days when the sons brought their wives to live with the family, and several generations lived together under one roof. Most modern Japanese apartments are overcrowded with the addition of a baby, and most parents are in no position to add an entire family to their living quarters. Walk down this path a bit further, and you find questions. Who will take care of elderly parents if their children are not in a position to do so? What impact will there be on the population if couples postpone or avoid having children at least in part because of space issues? Japanese even must question whether societal problems such as divorce and teen violence are exacerbated by the fact that one or both parents have to work long, hard hours to afford decent housing, leading to problems at home.

JAPANESE HISTORY IN BRIEF

Japan's past is reflected in its present, so to understand Japan today one must understand its history. Many books have been written specifically on the topic of Japanese history, but since that is not the purpose of this book, this section is limited to the highlights of Japanese history. If you plan to spend any significant amount of time in Japan, it would be a good idea to also pick up a book dedicated to the history of Japan.

Japan's history is shrouded in the mists of time. Shintō mythology says that Japan was created by the ancient lovers Izanagi-no-Mikoto and Izanami-no-Mikoto. The pair stood on the Floating Bridge of Heaven and dipped the Heavenly Jewelled Spear into the ocean. When they withdrew the spear, droplets of water fell back to earth and created the island of Onogoro-jima, where the lovers were married and Izanami gave birth to the islands of Japan. They also created the many other *kami,* or deities, such as the Sun Goddess Amaterasu and her brother, the Storm God Susano-o. Amaterasu's grandson, Ninigi, ruled over the islands, and it was his great-grandson, Jimmu, who was the first human emperor of Japan. Thus, the lineage of the imperial family was traced back to the divine.

Archeologists, on the other hand, say that the Japanese people are the result of immigration and intermingling of people from Korea, China, the South Pacific, and Siberia between 35,000 and 30,000 BC. The Jōmon Period is recognized as the first civilization for which there is recorded archeological evidence.

10,000–300 BC Jōmon Period

Pottery shards, decorated by pressing rope into the wet clay, dated to this time gave the Jōmon ("rope patterns") period its name. The people living at this time appear to be hunter-gatherers and fishermen.

300 BC–AD 300 Yayoi Period

The Yayoi period takes its name from an area of Tokyo where fragments of pottery were found. The people of this time developed cultivation of rice in irrigated, wet fields and learned to make tools and weapons from iron and bronze to replace their ancestors' stone implements.

300–710 Kofun Period

Burial mounds found in central and western Japan dating from the 300s provided the name for the Kofun ("old tomb") period. Scholars theorize that the practice of burying the dead in the large, elaborate mounds that define this period was put to an end by the arrival of Buddhism. The Kofun period marks a change from a largely tribal culture to one that was cohesive. A ruling class of aristocracy, largely based on military might, developed. The Japanese began looking outward and gained control of the southern part of the Korean peninsula.

710–794 Nara Period

Although brief in span, the Nara period saw a further coalescence of a centralized government and a huge increase in attention to administration. The custom prior to this period was to move the capital to a new location following the death of the emperor, since it was believed that the site of death was polluted. In 710, Nara was established as the permanent capital and became Japan's first urban center. However, the "permanent" capital was later moved to Nagaoka in 784 and to Heian, which later became known as Kyoto, in 794.

794–1185 Heian Period

Imperial authority began to erode as powerful families chose to ignore land distribution and tax systems imposed by the government. Power began to shift to noble families, the most powerful of which was the Fujiwara family. Japan developed culturally and artistically in this period with the addition of *kana* (a system of syllabic writing) to supplement the Chinese *kanji* (ideograms) that had long been in service. Literature and art flourished as Japan emerged from the shadow of China to form its own styles of writing and painting.

1185–1333 Kamakura Period

Decentralization of the government was almost complete by the beginning of the Kamukara period, with the imperial family and court playing a mostly ceremonial role. Real power was in the hands of the *bushi* (warrior) class. The most powerful of these was Minamoto Yoritomo, whose base was in Kamakura; his government is often referred to in Western resources as a shogunate because he had been given the title of *seii taishōgun* by the emperor. The Minamoto family never managed to bring all of Japan under its control, and on the death of Yoritomo, they gradually became figureheads, much like the emperor, and were replaced by the Hōjō family.

1333–1567 Muromachi Period

Kublai Khan had been leading attacks on Japan since 1274, and the cost of war had taken its toll, eventually leading to the downfall of the Kamakura and Hōjō families and bringing the Ashikaga family into

power in their wake. Ashikaga struggled with civil war and general unrest and it was several decades before order began to be restored. The balance of power shifted from the *shōgun* to *daimyō*, regional rulers whose power increased under the rule of Ashikaga Yoshimitsu.

1576–1600 MOMOYAMA PERIOD

The warring *daimyō* were brought in check by a handful of powerful military leaders. Dominant among these was Oda Nobunaga, who gained the support of the emperor and struck down opposition from

Buddhist monks and rival *daimyō*. After his assassination, he was succeeded by his general, Toyotomi Hideyoshi, who continued to increase his rule through both warfare and strategic alliances, reunifying Japan under military rule.

1600–1867 TOKUGAWA OR EDO PERIOD

Bushi rule continued unchallenged, with the reins held by Tokugawa Ieyasu. Although he did not gain complete control in all corners of Japan, his ruthless decimation of enemy families soon left him in virtual control of the country. The Tokogawa family oversaw more than two centuries of relative stability from their capital in Edo. The system evolved so that the *shōgun* ruled nationally, while the *daimyō* had authority regionally.

1868–1912 MEIJI PERIOD

The Meiji period, also called the Meiji Restoration, saw profound changes in Japan. Imperial power was returned to the emperor and the new government sought to make Japan a democratic state. Feudal lords were forced to turn their land over to the emperor and reforms transformed the education and military systems, as well as the economy. The government became directly involved in business, created the first constitution, and established a parliamentary system of government.

1889	Constitution of the Empire of Japan (the Meiji Constitution) created
1890	First national election held
1894–95	Sino-Japanese War

TWENTIETH CENTURY TO PRESENT

1904–05	Russo-Japanese War
1910	Japan completes total annexation of Korea
1912	Emperor Yoshihito takes the throne after his father, Emperor Meiji dies

1914–18	Japan sides with Allies in World War I, but plays only a minor role, fighting German troops in Asia
1923	Great Kantō Earthquake devastates Tokyo and Yokohama
1926	Emperor Hirohito gains the throne
1929	Along with the rest of the world, Japan enters into a period of economic depression
1937	Second Sino-Japanese War breaks out
1941	Japan launches surprise attack on Pearl Harbor after failed diplomatic attempts to secure U.S. neutrality
1945	U.S. drops nuclear bombs on Hiroshima and Nagasaki; Emperor Hirohito offers Japan's unconditional surrender and Japan is occupied by Allied forces
1946	Japan's new constitution is written, removing power from the emperor; Emperor Hirohito officially relinquishes his family's claim to divine origin
1952	Allied occupation of Japan ends
1972	U.S. returns Okinawa to Japan
1993	Liberal Democratic Party (LDP) defeated by a coalition of eight rival parties after nearly four decades as head of the government
1995	The Great Hanshin Earthquake decimates Kōbe; Aum Shinrikyō sect attacks Tokyo subway system with poisonous gas

NOTED (AND NOTORIOUS) JAPANESE

Japan's past and present are full of brave warriors, talented artists, great leaders, and a host of other colorful characters. The people listed below are not by any means the only important individuals in Japan; they are but a few representatives of the country's vast history. Although some of the people listed below are known to the outside world by the Westernized method of putting the family name last, they are listed in this section according to the Japanese tradition of placing the family name first, followed by the given name.

Historical Figures

SHŌTOKU TAISHI (574–622)
Prince Shōtoku was born to Emperor Youmei and one of his wives, Empress Anahobe-hashinohito. Following his father's death and an uncle's assassination, he became regent under his aunt, Empress Suiko. Prince Shōtoku sent Japan's first royal envoy to China and was responsible for importing many ideas from China and Korea. A devotee of Buddhism, Prince Shōtoku is credited as being instrumental in spreading Buddhism throughout Japan. Under his direction, many Buddhist temples were built, including the Hōryū-ji, the oldest in Japan.

TOKUGAWA IYEYASU (1543–1616)
Tokugawa Iyeyasu was born in a time of turbulence, amid clans struggling for power. Born Matsudaira Takechiyo, he spent much of his childhood as a prisoner of a rival family, then as a hostage given by his own family to cement their alliance with a neighboring clan. When he claimed leadership of the Matsudaira family, he changed his name to Tokugawa Iyeyasu and began building his dynasty. In 1603, he was given the title of *shōgun*. In 1615, he defeated the last of the rival clans, uniting Japan and ushering in more than 250 years of peace under Tokugawa rule.

ITŌ HIROBUMI (1841–1909)
A Japanese statesman during the Meiji period, Itō was instrumental in laying the foundations for the modern Japanese state. A visit to England to study science convinced the young Itō that Japan's future

lay in adopting some of the ways of the West. Itō went on to serve in the ministries of foreign affairs, finance, and industry. In 1871, he was part of a mission to revise unequal treaties with Western countries and to study Western technology. In 1873, Itō became a member of the ruling council, and by 1881, he held significant political clout. He helped shape the Japanese government using a model based on Western governments and supervised the drafting of the 1889 constitution. A supporter of government run by a party system rather than by the imperial family, Itō became the first president of the Seiyuki party and served as prime minister from 1892–1896, again in 1898, and from 1900–1901. In 1905, Ito pushed through an agreement with Korea that forced Korea to become a protectorate of Japan and moved to Korea to administer it. He was assassinated in 1909 while in Korea, leading the Japanese to subsequently annex Korea.

EMPEROR MEIJI (1852–1912)

Born with the given name of Mutsuhito in 1852, Emperor Meiji took his reign name when he ascended the throne in 1867 at the age of fifteen. In the following year, the shogunate fell, and the power that had been in the hands of the Tokugawa family was returned to the emperor. Thus began the Meiji Restoration. During this period, feudalism was replaced by a new state, which was the beginning of modern Japan. Although the emperor himself held little political power, he had tremendous presence and charisma and he was a symbolic figure in a time or restoration and renewal. Under his aegis, Japan's constitution was enacted and the two-house government system was put into place. It was under Emperor Meiji's reign that Japan began its transformation into an industrialized global power.

Business Leaders

MATSUSHITA KŌNOSUKE (1894–1989)

Born in a rural village, Matsushita rose to the forefront of Japanese industry. When Matsushita was nine years old, his father, a promi-

nent landowner, lost his property and Matsushita was forced to quit school and go to work to help support his family. Just after the turn of the century, electricity was beginning to make an appearance. Matsushita, recognizing its potential, sought a job at the Osaka Electric Light Company. In his spare time, Matsushita designed an improved light socket. Unable to convince the light company of its viability, he left to form his own small company, which over the years has grown and evolved into the conglomerate Matsushita Electric, encompassing a host of well-known names such as Panasonic and National.

In addition to his business success, Matsushita is renowned for his innovations not only in products, but in management practices as well. His was one of the first companies to establish a five-day workweek, a labor union, and employee training programs. The tale most often used to demonstrate his unique approach to business relates how Matsushita, in the early days of radio, purchased the patent rights to two key radio components and released them to the public domain in order to stimulate the growth of this exciting new industry. In 1947, Matsushita founded the PHP Institute, an organization that addresses fundamental issues concerning the human condition.

MORITA AKIO (1921–1999)

The son of a family with a four-hundred-year history of sake brewing, Morita left the family business after serving in World War II to found a company called Tōkyō Tsūshin Kōgyō (Tokyo Telecommunications Engineering Corporation) with Ibuka Masaru. In 1958, Morita was instrumental in changing the company's name. If they were going to enter the global market and be successful, they needed a name that would be easily recognized and remembered. Furthermore, that name should be written in *katakana*, the alphabet used to write foreign names. Thus, the Sony Corporation was born. In 1960, the Sony Corporation of America was founded, and in 1961, Sony became the first Japanese company to offer shares on the New York Stock Exchange.

KUROSAWA AKIRA (1910–1998)

Director Kurosawa Akira released his first film, *Sugata sanshirō*, in 1933. He caught the international spotlight when his film *Rashōmon* won an Oscar for Best Foreign Film in 1952. Subsequent films won numerous international awards. Kurosawa was awarded an honorary Oscar for lifetime achievement in 1990. Some of Kurosawa's movies were about the adventures of great warriors, such as the film *Seven Samurai*, replete with fierce battle scenes; others were tales of ordinary people living ordinary lives, told with simple realism.

MURASAKI SHIKIBU (C. 976–C. 1031)

Murasaki Shikibu was a Japanese novelist during the late Heian period. Her novel *Genji monogatari* (*The Tale of Genji*), is a masterpiece in the history of Japan, and is considered by many to be the first modern novel. In a time when girls were given only the most basic education, Lady Murasaki's discreet presence in the tutoring sessions her brother received allowed her to learn Chinese language and literature and other subjects. Married at age 20 and widowed soon thereafter, Lady Murasaki was invited to become lady-in-waiting Akiko, a consort of the Emperor Ichijō. It was during these years in court that she wrote the novel that she would be remembered by, and it's thought that much of it was based on the people and events in her own life.

TEZUKA OSAMU (1928–1989)

Tezuka Osamu was a medical student of eighteen when he began drawing a newspaper comic strip called *Ma-chan's Diary*. He soon began producing entire stories drawn as comics, bringing an almost cinematic quality to the art. He was instrumental in the development of Japanese *manga* (comics) in the 1950s and 1960s, introducing strong story lines and complex characters, even publishing *manga* versions of classics such as Dostoevsky's *War and Peace*. Tezuka has many famous pieces among his vast body of work, such as *Janguru taitei* (*Kimba, the White Lion*) and *Ribon no kishi* (*Princess Knight*), as well as many unforgettable characters.

Sports and Entertainment

FUTABAYAMA SADAJI (1912–1968)

One of Japan's legendary sumo wrestlers, Futabayama was the 35th *yokozuna* sumo. His debut as a sumo wrestler was in 1927, when he was fifteen years old; he was promoted to *yokozuna* in 1937. Between the years of 1936 and 1940, Futabayama won 69 consecutive bouts and won 12 *makunouchi* division championships.

MISORA HIBARI (1937–1989)

Misora, often called the queen of Japanese singers, is arguably the most famous *enka* (Japanese-popular-song) performer in Japan, having recorded more than 300 albums and appeared in more than 150 films. Born in Yokohama City, she started singing and performing locally as a child, debuting on a national scale in 1949. At a time when Japan was struggling to recover from the devastation of World War II, Misora's songs seemed to give hope where there was none, encouraging the country in a time of economic hardship.

Oh Sadaharu (1940–)

Oh Sadaharu signed with the Tokyo Yomiuri Giants baseball team in 1959. During his career, he hit 868 home runs, holding the all-time professional baseball record, surpassing Hank Aaron's record in 1978. Oh won 13 consecutive home run titles and 15 total career titles; he was voted the league's Most Valuable Player nine times. Following his retirement in 1980, Oh managed the Yomiuri Giants, then the Fukuoka Daiei Hawks. He was voted into the Japanese Baseball Hall of Fame in 1994.

RELIGION

The most prevalent religions in Japan are Shintō and Buddhism. It's important to note here that although we may refer to these as religions, they are more accurately described as philosophies or belief systems. As such, they are neither monotheistic nor mutually exclusive, as are religions such as Christianity, Judaism, and Islam. For this reason, no matter what they may label themselves, the Japanese are quite comfortable embracing the beliefs of both Shintō and Buddhism. In Japan, even members of another religion, such as Christianity, incorporate elements of Shintō and/or Buddhism into their belief systems, rites, and rituals.

There is a small minority of Christians—about 1%—in Japan, and an even smaller number of Muslims, who are mostly non-Japanese residing in Japan temporarily. There are also a small number of new religions and cults, legitimate and otherwise, that have formed in the past few decades. Superstition, myth, folklore, and Confucianism have also influenced the belief systems in Japan and deserve mention as well.

The Japanese are not, on the whole, an overtly religious people. On the other hand, many families have a Shintō or Buddhist shrine or altar in their homes and follow traditional religious rituals for annual festivals and life's milestones, such as weddings and funerals. In fact, in many homes you will see both a Shintō shrine and Buddhist altar. In the same spirit, it is common for someone to have a Shintō wedding, but a Buddhist funeral.

Shintō

Shintō is native to Japan, although its origin cannot be traced to a specific date or person. Shintō grew from the myths that explained the origin of Japan and the Japanese people; it also assigned a divine origin to the Imperial Family. Every element of nature, such as the sun and moon, wind and water, even rocks and trees had its own deity. Communities and households had guardian *kami* (gods) and heroes were deified. Prior to World War II, the emperor himself was considered a god; he lost his divine status during the American occupation of Japan following the war.

There is no canon or "Bible" for Shintō; its beliefs and tenets are much more indefinable. Infinitely more concrete are Shintō rituals, which begin with a newborn baby's first visit to a Shintō shrine. Various rituals and festivals are observed throughout the year and, indeed, throughout life. Shintō is also evident in everyday life. Examples are talismans to ward off evil, purification rites on things like the site where a building is to be built, and blessings for everything from a new car to a new home.

Buddhism

Buddhism was begun in India by Siddhartha Gautama, a prince turned teacher and philosopher. The name Buddha means "enlightened." The ideals of Buddhism focus on achieving freedom from the cycle of death and rebirth and thereby entering into Nirvana, perfect and total peace and enlightenment.

At the center of Buddhism lie the Four Noble Truths:

- Life is suffering
- Desire is the cause of suffering
- When you cease to desire, you eliminate suffering
- Desire, and thus suffering, can be eliminated by following the Middle Way and the Eightfold Noble Path

The Middle Way is exactly that: a way of life that exists between the wanton sating of desire and zealous self-denial. The Eightfold Noble Truths consist of right views, intention, speech, conduct, livelihood, effort, attention, and meditation.

Buddhism came to Japan in the mid sixth century by way of China and Korea. The influence of Buddhism—and through it, the Chinese culture—helped create a centralized state in Japan. Japanese Buddhism belongs to the Mahayana (Greater Vehicle) school, believing in salvation for everyone. (The second school, Hinayana or Lesser Vehicle, focuses on individual salvation.)

Buddhism has many subdivisions or schools of thought. Zen Buddhism gained prominence in Japan, although its origins are in India and China. Zen Buddhism itself has two different schools, each choosing a different path to enlightenment, one through *zazen* (seated meditation) and the other through *kōan* (riddles such as the monk Hakuin's question "What is the sound of one hand clapping?").

Buddhism found an easy partnership with Shintō, and each integrated parts of the other. Buddhist temples, for example, soon gained *kami* to protect the Buddha and the *kami* themselves were considered Bodhisattvas, who had found enlightenment but delayed entering Nirvana so that they could help others along the path. In this way, Shintō and Buddhism existed in harmony for centuries until Shintō was officially elevated during the Meiji period.

POLITICS AND GOVERNMENT

Japan is a constitutional monarchy. The emperor is a symbolic position; the prime minister is the active head of the government. Although he wields no political power, the Japanese emperor is nonetheless highly respected.

Japan has nine political regions: Hokkaidō, Tōhoku, Chūbu, Kantō, Kinki, Chūgoku, Shikoku, Kyūshū, and Okinawa. It is further divided into 47 administrative divisions, which include 43 *ken* (rural prefectures), two *fu* (urban prefectures: Kyoto and Osaka), one *to* (metropolitan district: Tokyo) and one *dō* (district: Hokkaidō). Each *ken* is subdivided into *shi* (cities), *gun* (counties), *mura* (villages) and *chō* (precincts). Tokyo, Kyoto, and Osaka, the *to* and *fu*, are subdivided into *shi*, *ku* (wards), and *chō*. Hokkaidō, Japan's single *dō*, is divided into *shicho* (subdistricts).

The Government System

Japan's parliamentary government takes the form of a bicameral legislature called the Kokkai (Nation Diet), which comprises the Shūgiin (House of Councillors or upper house) and the Sangiin (House of Representatives or lower house). General elections for the Sangiin are held every three years for alternating halves of the house seats. Members of the Shūgiin are elected every four years or when the House is dissolved.

The party with the most seats in the Kokkai appoints the prime minister, usually the party's president. The prime minister appoints his own cabinet, often selecting members entirely from the Kokkai.

Japan's civil law system is an independent series of courts consisting of a Supreme Court, high courts, district courts, and family courts.

Political Parties

Japan's leading political party is the Jiyuu Minshu Tō (Liberal Democratic Party, LDP), which has been in power virtually exclusively since its formation 1955. The LDP was created by the merger of two conservative parties formed after World War II. The LDP governed the country without interruption until the early 1990s, when the party became factionalized and eventually lost its parliamentary majority in 1993. Coalitions with other parties have allowed the LDP to keep a leading role in Japan's governance. The LDP charter states that protection of civil liberties, openness, and democracy are paramount; issues of global peace, prosperity, and preservation of the global environment are all stated as issues at the forefront of the LDP's agenda.

Japan's second largest party is the Minshu Tō (Democratic Party of Japan, DPJ), formed from a merging of various proletarian parties in existence before World War II. The party was built on the foundation of unarmed neutrality. However, it revised this platform following the formation of a coalition government with the LDP in 1994.

Minority parties include the Sakigake (Harbinger Party), Shinsei Tō (Renewal Party), both small, conservative parties created by a former LDP factions, Kōmei Tō (Clean Government Party), and the Japan New Party.

ECONOMY

Japan's economy was virtually paralyzed in the aftermath of World War II. Japan faced severe inflation and food shortages. Factories had been decimated by bombings, domestic demand decreased with demilitarization, and foreign trade was restricted by occupying forces. The Japanese, however, had one asset that was instrumental in rebuilding the economy from the ashes of war to the modern, thriving economy it is today: a nation of people who were willing to work long and hard, placing the needs of the country in front of their own interests.

Japan's economy is the third largest in the world, after the U.S. and China, and it is arguably the most technologically advanced economy in the world. Beginning in the mid-1970s, the bulk of Japan's economy was focused on exports. However, after a decade, the focus shifted back to the domestic market.

Japan has several unique characteristics that contribute to its success, the first of which is the dedicated work force mentioned above.

Keiretsu are another intrinsic part of the Japanese economy. These are a group of companies from different sectors whose interests are closely tied together; each company usually owns part of the other companies in the *keiretsu* and the business leaders sit on the boards of many of the companies. The ideal is to have one company in each major industry, such as real estate, manufacturing, technology, and banking, to protect the group from takeovers and provide it with leverage. Mitsubishi is the *keiretsu* that is probably the most well-known outside of Japan.

The government has long played a role in business in Japan, subsidizing and protecting industries. The fact that Japan spends only about 1% of its GDP on defense, a direct result of a prohibition on rearmament written into the new Constitution, didn't hurt, either.

Japan has historically been an environment of lifetime employment, which further stabilized both the society and the economy. However, in recent years, both the ideal of lifetime employment and the *keiretsu* business model have eroded.

Japan has little arable land, but the crops that are grown are heavily subsidized. Japan is a self-sufficient grower of rice and fish, but little else. Japan's real strength lies in industry, particularly high technology.

HOLIDAYS AND FESTIVALS

January 1	Ganjitsu (or Gantan) New Year's Day
January, 2nd Sunday	Seijin-no-hi (Coming-of-Age Day)
February 11	Kenkoku Kinem-bi (National Foundation Day)
March 21 or 20	Shumbun-no-hi (Spring Equinox)
April 29	Midori-no-hi (Greenery Day)
May 3	Kempō Kinem-bi (Constitution Day)
May 5	Kodomo-no-hi (Children's Day)
July 20	Umi-no-hi (Marine Day)
September 15	Keirō-no-hi (Respect for the Aged Day)
September 23 or 24	Shūbun-no-hi (Autumn Equinox)

October, 2nd Monday	**Taiiku-no-hi (Sports Day)**
November 3	**Bunka-no-hi (Culture Day)**
November 23	**Kinrō Kansha-no-hi (Labour**
	Thanksgiving Day)
December 23	**Tennō Tanjōbi**
	(Emperor's Birthday)

In addition to the national holidays, there are many other yearly rites, rituals, and festivals; some are celebrated on a national level and some are local or regional. Although these festivities are far too numerous to describe individually, following are some examples of events that occur throughout the year.

Ganjitsu (or Gantan) New Year's Day, January 1

New Year's Day is a day for tradition and for family. Many companies give their employees several days off for this holiday. Even people who leave their *kimono* in the closet 364 days of the year don them for this special day. Homes are decorated with *shime-nawa* hung at the front gate or entrance to ward off evil. *Kadomatsu*, made of bamboo stalks and pine branches tied together with straw, are placed on either side of the door to invite the *toshigami*, who brings wealth and good harvests. Inside the house is a *kagami-mochi*, made from two rice cakes stacked together, decorated and placed on the family altar or other place of honor. Temples and shrines are generally packed on this day since most families observe the tradition of *hatsu-mōde*, the year's first visit to the temple or shrine to pray for health, happiness, and prosperity. At home the family eats the foods that will bring fortune and luck, such as red snapper, since red is the color associated with luck. Children receive *otoshi-dama*, a small present to celebrate the new year, which nowadays is almost always money. Depending on where you find yourself on this day, you may also have the opportunity to witness some local New Year's Day customs, such as ancient games or contests played in period costume or special blessings at shrines.

Setsubun (last day of winter by the lunar calendar), February 3 or 4

Put soybeans on your grocery list the week before *setsubun*—roasted soybeans, symbolizing evil, are thrown out the door accompanied by everyone chanting "*Oni wa soto*" ("Out with the devil"). Japanese dads often put on a devil's mask, only to be thrown out of the house and pelted with soybeans. Then more soybeans are scattered throughout the house as you say "*Fuku wa uchi*" ("In with good luck!"). Be sure to set aside a few soybeans, since it's customary to eat the same number of soybeans as your age to guarantee a healthy year.

Hina Matsuri (Doll Festival), March 3

Hina are dolls that represent the ancient imperial court, including the Emperor and Empress and all of their attendants. Little girls often receive these dolls as a gift at their birth, usually from their grandparents. These dolls are set out on display for Hina Matsuri. The dolls you will see on display may range from a simple pair representing the imperial couple to a dozen tiers of dolls representing everyone from the Emperor to the court musician. If you are in Tokyo on this date, you can visit the Myōen-ji temple, where children dress in costumes from the royal court to create a live *hina* display. This traditional setting out of the dolls is meant to give thanks for the health and well-being for one's daughter(s).

Golden Week, April 29–May 5

If you like crowded trains, traffic that moves at a snail's pace, and standing shoulder-to-shoulder with thousands of other people at your favorite vacation spot, then by all means schedule a trip during Golden Week. Golden Week begins with Midori-no-hi (Greenery Day) on April 29 and passes through Kempō Kinem-bi (Constitution Day) on May 3 and ends with Kodomo-no-hi (Children's Day) on May 5. These are all national holidays, so when the calendar works in your favor, you can throw in one or two vacation days and have a ten-day holiday for the cost of a few vacation days. Many Japanese take advantage of the nearly consecutive holidays to schedule their family vacations, leaving railroads, highways, and tourist spots jam-packed with vacationers.

Kodomo-no-hi (Children's Day), May 5

Before World War II, May 5 was a day honoring boys, much as March 3 honors girls. However, it has been converted into Children's Day, honoring all children. On this day, families that have sons will fly carp-shaped banners or wind socks, symbolizing male strength.

They may also display the costume of a samurai warrior, or, if space is tight, perhaps just the helmet. The most opulent displays include full armor as well as miniature replicas of ancient weapons.

Bon Festival, August 13–16

Buddhists believe that the soul's of one's ancestors revisit their homes once a year during Bon. Different areas and even different families have their own ways of preparing to welcome their ances-tors. Some typical ceremonies include lighting a small fire outside the home on the first day of Bon to guide the spirits, a ritual cleaning of the home's Buddhist altar and erection of a special *shōryōdana* (spirit altar), and a visit by a Buddhist priest or monk. In many towns, dancing, song, and music welcome the spirits home. The spirits stay with their families for a few days, then are guided on their way back to the spirit world with another fire; in some areas, lanterns and offerings of food are set adrift on the river or sea. Since this is a very family-oriented celebration, many companies give their employ-ees a few days off so they can travel back to their home towns.

Christmas, December 25

Christianity is a minor religion in Japan—less than 1% of the popu-lation is Christian—but that doesn't stop the Japanese from celebrat-ing Christmas. Christmas is not a national holiday and, of course, not everyone celebrates Christmas, but those that do usually have a Christmas tree, a groaning table on Christmas Eve, and a visit from Santa Claus, who places presents near children's heads as they sleep.

Year-End Rituals, December

The Japanese version of "spring cleaning" takes place in December, as the home is thoroughly cleaned high and low to prepare for the new year. Good wishes for the new year are sent to friends and col-leagues by mail; if you get yours to the post office by mid-December, they will be held for a special delivery on January 1. Some people send more than a hundred new year's cards, which is indeed a daunting task. On New Year's Eve, families traditionally have a simple dinner of buckwheat noodles. The simplicity of the meal represents the ideal of a simple life and the length of the noodles is symbolic of hopes for a long life.

EDUCATION

Compulsory education in Japan is from grades one through nine (ages six through fifteen). Education at this level is free at public schools, although parents can elect to pay to send their child to a private school instead.

Although attendance is voluntary and is not free, the majority of children begin their education at preschool or kindergarten. Parents often register their children for preschool at the age of three.

Children begin their compulsory education in elementary school at age six and go through six years of elementary education. Following this is lower secondary school, which lasts three years. A teenager who has completed lower secondary school can leave, but fewer than 4% do.

A student who completes the next level of education, upper secondary school, which lasts three years, can take an exam to gain entrance to post-secondary school. About 45% of secondary school graduates continue on to post-secondary education. There are several types of post-secondary educational institutions, including four-year universities, two-year junior colleges, and technical or vocational schools. Finally, university students can elect to pursue post-graduate degrees in their area of study.

The Japanese value education and a degree from a top-notch university carries a lot of weight when one enters the work force. As a matter of fact, competition for entry into the best schools is quite stiff, starting at the preschool level and continuing through university entrance exams. As a result, numerous "cram schools" have sprung up. Parents send their children to these private schools, which provide students with supplementary instruction, in hopes of securing the child's place in the most prestigious schools.

Japan's public universities are very highly regarded; most are held in higher esteem than private institutions. Acceptance by a university is based almost solely on entrance exam scores. Students applying for entrance to a national university must take both a national uniform achievement test and a test administered by the university itself. Students applying to a private university need only take that institution's examination. Many students who are denied entrance to the school of their choice wait one year and take the test again, rather than apply to a lesser school. These students, called *rōnin*, spend the interim months studying for their next attempt at the entrance exam.

After school, children can attend *juku*, a special private school. One type of *juku* is the "cram school" mentioned above, with the specific goal of improving entrance exam scores. But other types of *juku* exist as well. For example, an academic *juku* may offer assistance for a student who is struggling with a particular subject or a subject that is not part of the school's curriculum. Nonacademic *juku* offer sports, such as swimming lessons, to cultural or artistic instruction, such as piano lessons. Although *juku* are not free, enrollment is rising, indicating that they play a major role in the Japanese education system, one that parents are willing to budget for.

Learning in a Japanese school is largely by rote, with the teacher or professor in the role of authority, rarely questioned by students. Academic performance is judged solely on the basis of examination. In addition to academic learning, schools are also expected to teach moral values and to develop character. Schools instill in their pupils a respect for society, societal order, and group goals instead of individual interests.

TWO

CULTURE

We all have programmed into us a certain code, a set of rules by which we live and interpret the world. These rules govern both our actions and our reactions. They are instilled in us by our parents, our teachers, and our peers. Culture, then, is the combined values, beliefs, mores, motivations, and attitudes that shape our view of the world.

Though we are all individuals, we are all influenced by the culture in which we grow up. Despite our individual differences, there are nevertheless cultural ties that bind us together. No matter how little someone from Des Moines thinks he has in common with a New Yorker, they are indeed more similar to each other than to someone from Tokyo or Riyadh.

This chapter explores the cultural differences between Japan and the United States. Although endless distinctions can be made between cultures, here we break culture down into six different categories that will paint a practical, accessible portrait of Japanese culture viewed through American eyes. These categories are: time, communication, group dynamics, status/hierarchy, relationships, and reasoning. Each section begins with a brief overview of the category and its polar opposites. As we explore the category in more depth, we will take a look at where Japan and the U.S. fall on the continuum and how they relate to each other. By the end of the section, you should have a greater understanding of what may cause cultural misunderstanding and an idea of the very real challenges communicating across cultures can present. Finally, we will provide you with some tips to help you apply this information to your daily interactions with the Japanese. We will use this knowledge as we take a step-by-step look at the Japanese business culture in later chapters.

With any luck, you will emerge with a better understanding not only of what makes the Japanese tick, but of what makes you tick as well. Only when you are able to understand that cultural differences are neither bad nor good, merely different ways to look at the same reality, can you begin to build the cross-cultural skills you will need to be successful in Japan—or anywhere else in the world.

The following observations are of necessity painted in broad brush strokes. It is naturally unwise to think that every Japanese will behave in one way, and every American in another. However, there is enough evidence to support the idea that the Japanese as a culture tend to have certain preferences, as do Americans. Keeping that in mind, the information in this chapter will give you a foundation on which to lay the bricks of individual characteristics and personalities.

TIME

Chad Preston sat at his desk, frowning at yet another agenda for an upcoming meeting. After three months in Japan, Chad was beginning to feel like all he did was attend an endless string of useless meetings. His department had a standing meeting every other day. As a newly-arrived expatriate, Chad had willingly attended the staff meetings,

since he wanted to make sure he was kept in the loop on his projects. However, after a couple of weeks, Chad decided that he could get by with attending only the Monday morning meetings. After all, the only thing they ever did at the meetings was get a quick report of what everyone was doing. The rest of the time, it seemed, was spent on mutual back-patting. No one ever brought up any new ideas and Chad certainly had better things to do with his time.

Although there may be many reasons why Chad felt that the meetings he had to attend in his new position were a waste of his time, this scenario demonstrates that Chad has a very different view of where to budget his time than his Japanese counterparts. If Chad continues to skip meetings, in essence putting his time needs before other needs of his team, he risks offending his co-workers and being branded a poor team player.

Rigid Versus Flexible Cultures

Perhaps the first cultural challenge people encounter, often subconsciously, when they meet another culture is a difference in the perception of time. Time is a resource that different cultures view in different ways. We all have different answers to the questions "What is the value of time?" and "How is time best spent?" In the most basic terms, time can be either flexible or rigid.

In a rigid-time culture, the clock is the measure against which all of our actions are judged: whether we are saving time or wasting it, whether we are on time or late. People in rigid-time cultures like to plan their activities and keep a schedule. It is rude to show up late and important not to waste other people's time. Time is a commodity that must be spent wisely, not frittered away.

The clock for flexible-time cultures is more fluid, and things can happen more spontaneously. Plans are made, but with the understanding that they may be changed, even at the last minute, depending on circumstances. Punctuality is not a virtue, and many things can take precedence over adherence to a schedule.

Japanese-American Interaction

When an American is first introduced to Japan, he or she may feel that there is little difference in the countries' general perception of time. The etiquette books say that one should be on time to appointments in Japan, trains keep almost obsessively to a rigid schedule and, after all, aren't the Japanese the originators of the idea of "just-in-time" technology? A closer look at the two cultures, however, reveals that there is, in fact, a very real gap in perceptions of time.

In the U.S., time is money and efficiency is equated with speed. The pace of life is hectic as we rush from appointment to appointment, from home to work to the gym. Every moment of the day is closely scheduled and the proliferation of laptops, cellular phones, and other devices means that even the time spent getting from here to there is packed full of "doing."

In Japan, the ideas of maintaining harmony, nurturing relationships, and working as a cohesive group are valued above a fast pace. The differences manifest in many ways, especially in business. For example, as demonstrated in the scenario above, in a Japanese company, you may find that you are expected to attend weekly or even daily meetings that seem to have no purpose to an outsider; there may not even be any official business discussed. To an American, this would seem to be a waste of time, but to a Japanese it is a way of keeping a good working environment, creating "good vibes," if you will.

A further example of the different perceptions of time is found in the decision-making process. In Japan, decisions tend to take a long time to be made, since much time is spent making sure that everyone in the affected group agrees. In the U.S., conversely, decisions are made quite rapidly and more time is spent in implementing the decision. Overall, Japanese value the needs of the group over speedy decisions, whereas Americans value the ability to make decisions quickly.

Given these differences, it is not uncommon for the Japanese to feel that their American counterparts run roughshod over them and their feelings in the rush to get things done. Americans, on the other hand, often feel frustrated at the "time-wasting" processes of the Japanese.

Tips on Time

- Be on time for both business appointments and social occasions. If you are going to be late, make every effort to call ahead.
- Remember that as a rule, time takes a backseat to harmony and relationships. Impatience will get you nowhere.
- If you are doing business with Japanese, build more time into your schedule. Plan to spend time initially forging relationships; once that is accomplished, expect things such as decision-making to take longer. (See the chapter on Business Step-by-Step for more on these topics.)

CULTURE

COMMUNICATION

Grace Turner was on the telephone with Shinsuke Hashimoto. After discussing an idea for implementing a new quality control program, Grace wanted to get a timeline down on paper. "So, Shinsuke, you'll get me the customer service statistics for the past four quarters by the end of the day tomorrow, right?" she said. There was a long pause at the other end of the line, and Grace wondered if they had somehow been disconnected. "Hello? Shinsuke?" she prompted. Finally, Hashimoto replied. "I will try," he said hesitantly. "Great. I'll talk to you on Wednesday, then, after I get your report," Grace replied firmly. On Wednesday morning, Grace came into the office to find her "IN" box empty. Great, she thought as she snatched up the phone with irritation, once again Shinsuke didn't do what he said he was going to do. Didn't he know that when he didn't come through, it put her in a bind?

Direct Versus Indirect Communication

Direct Versus Indirect Communication

What is the goal of communication? Regardless of what culture you are from, you need to be able to relay information to other people. But is that the goal in and of itself, or are there other variables that affect that goal?

In cultures that value direct communication, the goal of communication is mainly to relay information. Value is placed on being able to state your point in a clear and concise manner, and words have limited nuances. In general, people do not appreciate having to pull the real point out from a surfeit of words.

If you are an indirect communicator, on the other hand, you have to take other factors into account. It may be important not to cause offense to your listener, to show deference, or to maintain harmony, for example. Very often the real meaning in indirect communication cultures is a subtext buried under many layers of meaning or intertwined with non-verbal clues or metaphors.

Japanese-American Interaction

Americans prefer to speak directly. "Don't beat around the bush" and "Get to the point," say Americans. Their Japanese counterparts, on the other hand, tend to be more circumspect. There are two very important precepts in the Japanese culture that make indirect communication preferable: *wa*, or harmony, and face. Unfortunately, these are the antithesis of American perceptions, making communication styles a hurdle to successful interaction.

In the U.S., there is nothing wrong with conflict and it's preferable to hash out problems openly. Differing opinions are beneficial, since they lead to discussion and often to new ideas. In contrast, in Japan it is essential to maintain harmony, or *wa*. Open conflict or contradictions that disturb the harmony are unwelcome.

The Japanese are under a lot of pressure to maintain "face." Most Westerners have some understanding of what this means, but it is limited by other characteristics of Western culture that define it. The desire to avoid embarrassment is universal; however, when and why one should be embarrassed is not.

Face, in its Eastern form, is a responsibility between two people that requires participation by both parties. There are many different aspects of face. Westerners are usually familiar with "losing face" and "saving face." But in the Western view, both of these ideas are seen in a more individualistic perspective; they all revolve around the self. A person loses or saves his or her own face; others are involved only in the role of the audience in front of whom this small drama occurs. In Japan, there is much more to face—face becomes an interactive exercise. An individual's motivation moves from the selfish protection of his or her own image to include the desire to enhance and protect the prestige of others.

Face has a direct impact on the way we communicate. In a society which values face, it becomes important that one not deliberately offend or insult the person with whom one is speaking. This would negatively impact the face of both parties. Therefore it becomes important to maintain harmony among people and avoid open conflict. This is best accomplished with an indirect approach to communication.

The American preference for direct communication and the Japanese need to be indirect are often at the root of conflict between the two cultures. Americans frequently feel that they can't get a "straight answer" from the Japanese, who in turn can be offended by what they perceive as rudeness on the Americans' part.

Tips on Communication

Remember that the Japanese have an indirect style of communication. Be careful not to speak too bluntly.

- Do not underestimate the importance of "face." Make it a point to keep face and to maintain the face of others.
- Most Japanese prefer not to say "no" outright. Learn to properly interpret the meaning behind phrases such as "Perhaps" and even "Yes."

- Choose your words and tone of voice to maintain wa, or harmony. It is usually counterproductive to lose your temper or shout.

GROUP DYNAMICS

Recently promoted to head of global sales, Louis Montgomery was making it a point to visit all of the regional offices, starting with Tokyo. To prepare for his trip, Louis had reviewed the office's sales reports and was pleased to see that sales had been increasing steadily over the past few years. The regional sales manager had gathered his sales staff together to meet Louis. After congratulating the group on their past efforts, Louis said that he thought a few people deserved special recognition. "I apologize in advance if I don't pronounce this right, but where is Takeo Ishizaki." The room was silent, so Louis repeated, "Takeo Ishizaki? Can you please stand up?" After several

more moments of silence, Ishizaki reluctantly rose and stood there looking down. Louis praised Ishizaki for bringing in the most sales in the past quarter and urged the rest of the group to follow Ishizaki's lead to make this quarter the best yet.

At the end of the quarter, Louis reviewed the new sales report. He was surprised to see that sales were down overall. However, most disappointing was the fact that Takeo Ishizaki, the shining star in the last quarter, had returned his lowest sales figures ever.

In trying to encourage his sales staff, Louis is using a method that works for him at home. He has singled out the person who has the best sales record for recognition, expecting that this preferential treatment will motivate the rest of the staff to perform better so that they, too, can bask in the spotlight. Although he may not make the connection, his tactics have the opposite effect. With a bit of knowledge about how group dynamics differ in Japan, he may have chosen a different motivational tack.

Group-Oriented Versus Individualistic

In the overall scheme of things, which is stronger: the needs of the individual or the needs of the group? Is it usually the case that individuals are willing to make sacrifices for the good of the group, or will the group suffer for the benefit of the individual?

We are all faced at one time or another with making a decision to place someone else's needs before our own—our family, our friends, our team at work. Where the deeper cultural differences lie, however, is in the expectations of society. What is the societal norm for looking out for oneself or one's group? The next time you stay late at the office, think about your motives for doing so. Are you really staying to finish the project because it will be an enormous benefit to your company? Or are you staying because in order to advance up the ladder of success it is important that you be perceived as dedicated and hardworking?

Groups can take on many forms. Your group might consist of your family (immediate or extended), coworkers, the company you work for, friends with whom you grew up and went to school, a tribe or clan, a religious group, or a local, regional, or national affiliation. And of course you may belong to many different groups throughout your life.

If you are group-oriented, the group is an inherent part of your identity. You are first and foremost Japanese or Muslim or Bantu or a member of the Fuentes family, and a major factor in your decisions and actions is how they affect other members of your group. As an individual you are much more inclined to align your own goals with that of the group. Your talent is part of a larger pool, and when you cooperate with others it becomes possible to reach a mutual goal.

For example, some of the sales people in your division brought in more revenue and some less. However, the important thing is that the sales goals were met, so everyone should share equally in the annual bonus. In this way, individual weaknesses are balanced by others' strengths so that a balance is achieved. The success of the team will strengthen it and encourage people to strive for higher goals.

The sales scenario wherein everyone shares equally in the bonus when some people have brought in more business than others seems unfair in individualistic cultures. Sure, it's great that we met our sales goal, but since I was responsible for proportionally more revenue than the other members of the team, I should receive a proportionate share of the annual bonus. If everyone got an equal share of the bonus, people would be tempted to coast along and not put maximum effort into their jobs. As a member of an individualistic culture, it is important that everyone receives the recognition due him or her and, conversely, that everyone takes responsibility for his or her mistakes.

A culture's inclination toward the group or the individual will be an important influence in areas such as teamwork, rewards and motivation, and decision-making.

Japanese-American Interaction

Americans pride themselves on their individualism. They like to be different, to stand out in a crowd. They are ingrained with the notion that each person should be responsible for his own actions. From infancy, American children are encouraged to make their own choices. When they grow up, many move far away from home. This mobility does not create an environment in which closely-knit extended families or groups of friends can survive. Instead, it fosters a strong sense of individuality.

On the other side of the group-individual continuum are the Japanese, an extremely group-oriented culture. Whereas Americans say that "the squeaky wheel gets the grease," the Japanese feel that "the nail that sticks up gets hammered down." In other words, one succeeds not by touting one's own accomplishments but by integrating into the group and moving forward as a whole.

The implications of the difference between how Americans and Japanese view the group and the individual are many. One example is seen in how teams work. In the U.S. a team is made up of individuals who work toward the same goal by taking parallel paths, while a Japanese team travels the same road together. The preference for putting the group before the individual means that Americans and Japanese have different approaches when it comes to decision-making, motivating, and managing. As a result, Americans are often impatient at the time it takes to get things done; they may also feel underappreciated, since their individual efforts are not recognized. On the other side of the coin is the Japanese, who often find Americans boastful and arrogant for "tooting their own horns." They can also feel pressured by Americans who are pushing for things to be done quickly or embarrassed when the spotlight falls directly on them.

Tips on Group Dynamics

- Work with the group, not against it. When meeting with Japanese, expect to give them time to process topics as a group without expecting an immediate response.
- Many people are reluctant to voice an individual opinion, especially in front of a superior. If you wish to incorporate individual initiatives, such as freely offering ideas in a brainstorming session, be sure you lay the groundwork first. Expect that it can

take a considerable amount of time to implement such a plan.

- Realize that people's priorities and expectations may be different from yours because of group dynamics. Take time to observe and understand how the Japanese groups you encounter function, be they a negotiating team, coworkers, or employees.

STATUS AND HIERARCHY

Greg Newman felt a distinct chill in the room, but he wasn't sure why. Greg, a projects manager, his assistant manager, and the marketing manager had traveled from Atlanta to Tokyo to discuss a project that was soon to be launched in partnership with a Japanese company. The groundwork had already been laid, or so

Greg thought. But here they were, in Tokyo, and nothing seemed to be happening. From the moment they had touched down, things had gone wrong. On their first day there, they had met with the Japanese company's vice president, accompanied by, it seemed, virtually every person in the rank and file of the Japanese company. Everyone had been so solemn, and Greg had tried to lighten the atmosphere by being friendly, but the Japanese were not cooperating.

It seems likely that Greg has run into some problems with different values of status and hierarchy. Greg's—and his company's—actions reflect a culture that is not very concerned about hierarchy. The team consists of only the people necessary to get the job done. The Japanese company, on the other hand, has presented a team headed by a vice president. Sending such a high-ranking person is symbolic of how much they value the partnership. Their perception is likely to be that the American company is less than fully committed to the partnership, since they sent no one above middle management. Greg has probably exacerbated the problem in his attempt to be friendly. It's likely that Greg's methods for this included trying to create an informal atmosphere by using people's first names and drawing everyone into the conversation. Unfortunately, these techniques are out of place in a more rigid hierarchical setting, resulting in Greg further undermining his cause.

Ascribed Versus Achieved Status

Social strata are inherent in all cultures. How we differ is in the way that we gain and attribute status. Do we acquire status by virtue of who we are or by what we do?

Status can be based on the inherent characteristics of a person, over which we have no control, such as age, race, gender, or family background. Or it may be based on what a person has accomplished, including educational and professional qualifications, such as the school one attended or whether one is a sign painter or a doctor.

Certainly, when we evaluate other people, we use a mixture of these criteria. However, a culture will generally value one over the other. In an ascribed-status culture, for example, an employee must show competence in order to advance in his or her job; however, he or she must also have seniority. The wisdom and experience that come with age are valued. Similarly, a manager might be influenced in his or her hiring decisions by the applicant's family background or social connections—or lack thereof. Social strata are generally well-defined and one does not easily move between them.

It is much more common in achieved-status cultures to accord status based on accomplishments. Social strata are less defined and it is not uncommon to move up the social ladder. While there are certain benefits that come with seniority, it is certainly possible for younger employees to be promoted above their elders. A person's past and, perhaps more importantly, future performance is valued above age. Many U.S. companies, in fact, have a certain number of "fast track" employees who are expected to move up quickly through the ranks based on their potential performance.

Vertical Versus Lateral Hierarchy

Another aspect of status is whether the hierarchical structure is vertical or lateral. Hierarchy is something that exists in all cultures, whether hidden or overt.

In a vertical hierarchy, the structure tends to be overt. Positions within the hierarchy, corporate or social, are clearly outlined, and it is expected that people show and receive the respect due to them as a result of their position within the hierarchy. This respect is shown in many ways, from the use of titles to the depth of one's bow to the vocabulary one uses. The expatriate manager who tries to get his subordinates to call him "Dave" in a vertical hierarchy probably isn't going to have much luck—his employees will feel uncomfortable using such a disrespectfully familiar form of address to their boss. The title "Mr. Dave" may be the closest his subordinates come to using his first name.

Lateral hierarchies allow more equality among colleagues. Each person must be respected for his or her ability, regardless of position in the company. The more egalitarian nature of lateral hierarchies usually means a more informal environment. Lateral hierarchies also allow for greater empowerment at lower levels, as most decisions related to their jobs are made by employees themselves; there is less direct instruction from superiors. There is less concern for following the exact lines of authority than there is for finding the person who is in a position to take care of the issue at hand. Therefore, an employee who needs information from someone in another part of the business would have the freedom to approach that person directly, rather than channeling the request up through his boss, then on to the other person's boss, and finally down to the person who has the information, a restriction that an employee in a hierarchical organization would find difficult to circumvent.

You will find that a culture's views of the nature and importance of status influence the relationship between superiors and subordinates, determining how information flows (or does not flow), how decisions are made, and how people move up through the ranks.

Japanese-American Interaction

Japan has a long history of hierarchy, stretching back to the times of feudal lords. The Japanese culture has also seen the influence of Confucianism, which stresses appropriate behavior based on relative status. That is not to say that the Japanese do not consider themselves as equals as human beings; they do. However, there remains a social and business hierarchy based on many things, such as age and position within a company. These differences should be appropriately acknowledged when people interact. Thus the boss is addressed by his title and respect is given to elders and the wisdom they have accumulated.

The U.S., on the other hand, prides itself on equality, even if reality often betrays this pride. Accomplishments are what make the man (or woman) and more respect is given to those who have had to create their own fortune than to those who have had things handed to them on a silver platter. Therefore, in the U.S., the boss is addressed as "Bill" or "Janice" and young superstars rise quickly.

This has many implications when one culture meets the other. Communication styles, management styles, information flow, and promotions are areas that are directly affected by a culture's view of status and hierarchy.

An American working in a traditional Japanese company may feel that he is not sufficiently rewarded for his performance, as he can seem to do no more than plod along a well-worn path up the ranks. A young person thrust into a Japanese environment after attaining a level above his Japanese counterparts may encounter difficulty establishing authority with his Japanese coworkers. He may also face resentment from older workers who must work for someone younger and less experienced. In addition, the Japanese environment, where one is forced to be eternally formal, may seem cold and unfriendly to an American.

Conversely, a Japanese person encountering an American environment for the first time is likely to feel uncomfortable with the lack of respect implied by the informal atmosphere. He may also find it difficult to manage people older than himself and have difficulty asserting his authority.

Tips on Status and Hierarchy

- It is important to show respect for status and hierarchy in Japan. Do not use anyone's first name unless invited to do so. As a default, you should always address people by their last name and "-san."
- Even if you call your friend "Yoshi" in the bar after work, be sensitive to changes in environment that necessitate more formality. For instance, when you and Yoshi go to visit an important client, you may need to temporarily switch to "Ito-san."
- You must also respect the hierarchy when it comes to getting things done. Follow the proper channels and don't jump lines of authority.

RELATIONSHIPS

Jo Barnes felt in her gut that the negotiations were just not going well. It had seemed like a good match. The Japanese company needed a supplier and her company needed buyers. However, she and her colleague had been in Japan for two days already, and the negotiations seemed to be stalling. The Japanese kept pestering her for details of little relevance. She had already given them chapter and verse of her company's history. Now it seemed as though all they wanted to do was talk aimlessly. Whenever Jo tried to bring the conversation back to the specifications of the contract, they reacted by dragging her off to dinner. She needed to get a signature on the contract, but was starting to wonder if the Japanese were stalling because they didn't want to follow through.

In a situation like the one described here, where two companies are about to embark on a partnership, it's not out of character for the Japanese representatives to want to establish a relationship first, both by getting to know Jo's company and Jo herself. Jo, however, feels impatient with this delay, feeling the need to get everything put on paper before they move on to getting to know one another.

Relationship-Oriented Versus Task-Oriented

In the business of life, what takes the priority: your personal relationships or the tasks you do? If you are from a relationship-oriented culture, relationships come before tasks, and, in fact, may be necessary in order to perform tasks. This can have many implications. A sickness in the family (even the extended family) may take precedence over work; a chance meeting with a friend might delay a scheduled meeting; a deal might not be struck until both parties have had time to build a basis of mutual respect and trust. Relationships—ones that go beyond just working together—are the cornerstones of a life of interdependent networks and are a goal in and of themselves.

Task-oriented folks, on the other hand, tend to focus on the job at hand and leave the relationships to whatever time is left over after the work is finished. No friendship or personal intimacy is necessary to perform one's job and it is generally considered more professional not to let one's personal life intrude on one's work. The general rule is that one should get on with one's business and worry about "being friends" later.

This is not to say that relationship-builders don't get things done; nor is it meant to imply that task-focused people are not friendly. It simply means that the expectations one has in one's personal and business relationships might not be the same as what is expected in another culture. If you are doing business abroad, you will find that these differences can be crucial to your success. You will see them crop up in negotiating, making deals, getting information, making sales, joint ventures and team, to name but a few areas.

Japanese-American Interaction

Building relationships is crucial in Japan. Relationships are the essential tool needed to get things done. Relationships start in school, at the university, and when one becomes part of a new "class" entering a company upon graduation. These relationships are nurtured and strengthened as each person receives and reciprocates favors, building a net of obligation for both parties. Mr. Fumiko, a university professor, went to grammar school with Mr. Hashimoto, so when Mr. Hashimoto's son wants to attend his university, Mr. Fumiko helps him secure a position. A few years later, when Mr. Hashimoto's company needs to hire a consultant, he pulls some strings to get Mr. Fumiko the job. In this way debts are created, repaid, and recreated, cementing the relationship between the two.

Relationships in the U.S. are much more tenuous and tend to be compartmentalized. Personal and business relationships are usually kept separate. Business relationships may or may not form after the initial deal is done; it's certainly not necessary to have an existing relationship with someone in order to do business. In addition, Americans like to keep an arm's-length distance dividing business and personal relationships. Although it wouldn't be true to say that they don't exist, nepotism and favoritism are frowned on. Therefore, if the university professor in the scenario above were an American—let's call him Mr. Smith—he would probably be careful to make sure his involvement could not be viewed as playing favorites. He might make sure that Mr. Jackson's son got his papers in on time and even provide a recommendation, but he would view it as the son's responsibility to get accepted on the merits of his grades and skills. Likewise, when Mr. Jackson's company was in need of a consultant, he would throw Mr. Smith's name into the hat, perhaps talk him up a bit, but Mr. Smith would have to prove he was the best choice; the decision would probably not be made on the basis of his acquaintance with Mr. Jackson.

Since the Japanese value relationships and Americans place more emphasis on getting things done, problems can arise when the two cultures meet. To an American it may seem that he cannot get his foot in the door or that his Japanese colleagues presume too much upon their friendship. A Japanese in an American environment may be disappointed to find that although the Americans seem so friendly on the surface, he does not really feel a close bond with anyone.

Tips on Relationships

- Don't expect to get things done quickly until you have established a mutual trust and respect. Because relationships are important in Japan, it follows that you will have to invest time in building them.
- Try to keep the balance of the relationship roughly equal. For example, if you consistently expect a friend or colleague to do favors for you, but you are unwilling to reciprocate, there is an imbalance in the relationship, which will be keenly felt.
- There are many different types of relationships in Japan. Because Japan is also a hierarchical culture, not all relationships are those of peers. For example, if you are a manager, you may find that you are expected to act almost as a parent to your subordinates at times. As the senior person in these relationships, your obligations will be greater.

REASONING

Hank Greene was getting more than a little impatient with his colleague, Takeo Honna. Honna, Greene felt, just wasn't pulling his weight. Honna and Greene had started with the company at the same time, Greene in the U.S. and Honna in Japan. When Greene arrived in Japan as part of a management exchange program, he had assumed that Honna was a star in the Japanese office, since he had his own office. However, after just a few months, Greene became acutely aware that he was doing all the work while Honna just hung around. Greene's resentment of Honna continued to build. Why, he wondered, did the Japanese management continue to promote Honna instead of getting rid of him, when he obviously wasn't capable of doing the job?

To Hank's way of thinking, Honna was reaping rewards that he did not deserve. In his view, job performance should have a direct impact on one's position in the company. In essence, outstanding performance results in promotion, poor performance results in getting canned. In Japan, however, there is much more that must go into this mix, such as the impact on overall morale and company loyalty. Is the cost of carrying a few non-achievers greater than the cost of losing the trust and loyalty of the other employees? The above scenario exemplifies the significant differences in the two approaches to reasoning.

Pragmatic, Analytical, or Holistic Reasoning

Perhaps the most complex manifestation of culture is found in our thought processes. Around the world the way people reason can be divided into three general styles: pragmatic, analytical, or holistic.

Pragmatic thinkers begin with the goal and seek the steps that will enable them to attain that goal. The emphasis is therefore on finding practical ways to solve a problem or reach a goal. For example, if the goal is to increase sales by 10% in a given year, the task is then to identify the means of doing so. A pragmatic thinker will, for example, compile information on increasing his or her client base and the purchases made by current clients. The pragmatic thinker's final report might include a brief mention of all of the ideas which were presented, but its most prominent point will be the recommendation of certain sales strategies and how best to implement these strategies.

Analytical thinkers take the reverse approach, focusing on the process with the goal as the logical conclusion. So an analytical thinker's approach to the problem above of increasing sales by 10% will be different. He or she will begin by exploring all options, including increasing client base and increasing purchases. From there the analytical thinker will select the strategies that will be the most beneficial, leading to the conclusion that it is possible to increase sales by 10% in a given year. This increase then becomes the goal.

Holistic thinkers incorporate both of the methods above, but they also tend to include elements in their thinking that most pragmatic and analytical thinkers would not. In determining sales, a holistic thinker would examine the information gathered on the potential and current client base, but he or she might also add a few things to the mix. For example, a holistic thinker may ask, what are the possibilities of expanding the current range of products? Even if the pragmatic and analytical thinkers above had thought of this scenario, it is much more likely to be in a linear fashion. That is, a seller of office products who is not a holistic thinker would not get into selling, say, women's lingerie. Holistic thinkers tend to be more non-linear in their thinking and may see a relationship between office products and women's lingerie that pragmatic and analytical thinkers do not, such as the fact that they have a ready supplier of both. Another example of a potential question asked by a holistic thinker is what the impact on the sales staff would be. Will the higher quotas require them to work more hours in the week or spend more time away from their families? Finally, after putting all of the pieces in the puzzle, the holistic thinker will see that it is possible to increase sales by 10%.

As you can see, each of the three scenarios above ended up in the same place: a 10% increase in sales. However, the road taken in each instance traveled through different terrain, different countries, even. This difference in reasoning styles has an unmistakable impact on doing business abroad. Its significance is readily apparent in the process of decision-making, of writing reports and making presentations, and even in communicating.

Japanese-American Interaction

Americans tend to be pragmatic thinkers, relying on a direct cause-and-effect relationship. The Japanese thought processes are generally more holistic. Examples of how the two cultures think differently can be found by looking at their respective businesses. Although there are a few exceptions to this rule, American companies tend to focus on being the best at one thing. IBM makes computers, and Coke makes soda. Although peripheral businesses might be added or created, they are almost always closely related to the main business. In Japan, however, many companies have divisions that seem to have no obvious relationship to one another. Yamaha makes musical instruments and motorcycles; *keiretsu* (conglomerates) such as Mitsubishi own everything from automobile manufacturing plants to real estate companies.

From an American perspective, the Japanese can get bogged down in what appear to be non-essentials, leading to unnecessary delay. Of course, the opposite applies as well: To the Japanese eye, the American thought process can seem decidedly narrow and often simplistic.

Tips on Reasoning

- Because Japanese processes are holistic, many things simply take more time. More people are consulted for their approval, and tweaking of ideas is done upfront before a final decision is made. (See the section on *Ringi Sho* and *Nemawashi* in Decision-Making in the Business Step-by-Step chapter for more details.)

- Don't forget that there are many peripheral aspects at play in the Japanese thought process. Wrapped up in reasoning styles are the other cultural ideas presented, such as relationships, group dynamics, and status.

WHAT DOES IT ALL MEAN?

As you have probably already noticed, there are often correlations between the above categories. None of the six categories exists in a vacuum. If relationships are more important to you, it follows that you will be more willing to spend time (or waste it, from a task-oriented point of view) getting to know people before plunging into the task; relationship-oriented cultures tend to also be flexible time cultures. Similarly, if strong and harmonious relationships are your goal, that will be reflected in the way you communicate; relationship-oriented cultures also tend to be indirect communication cultures. You see the pattern.

Japan is a complex culture and one that, since it sits virtually opposite the United States in each of the six cultural categories, is often difficult for Americans to understand. While Americans value time, direct communication, pragmatic thinking, and so on, the Japanese value relationships, a sense of structure, and a more encompassing viewpoint.

These are the obstacles you and your company must overcome. With knowledge, practice, and, most of all, respect for the Japanese culture, you can learn to modify your cultural perspective, and even your business practices in order to ensure a mutually beneficial relationship with your Japanese business colleagues and friends.

THREE

LIVING ABROAD

Most people face an international move with a combination of excitement and apprehension. Moving within the confines of your home country can be difficult enough; moving across borders adds a whole new dimension of cultural differences which can magnify the stress we all naturally feel in a new environment.

The single most important thing that you can do to ensure a successful sojourn abroad is to have realistic expectations. Unfortunately, it's difficult to gauge how realistic your expectations are before you go. You can, however, help define your perspective by considering the following points.

- **What do you hope to get out of your stay abroad?** If you will be working while you're abroad, your company will have certain expectations about the goals of your job, but it is up to you to set your own goals for personal and professional development. Be specific. Although "broadened horizons" is an admirable goal, "gaining an understanding of the domestic automotive market" is a marketable skill that you will be able to use. If you will not be employed, it is essential that you make plans now for how you will occupy your time in the new country. What skills and interests do you have that you can apply to your advantage? You will have many options, including volunteering, continuing your education, and developing a hobby or skill into a freelance business.

- **If you have a partner and/or children, are you starting out with a sound relationship with your partner and with your children?** Although it may be tempting to regard an international assignment as a time to make a fresh start, it is not advisable to use the assignment to try to mend a troubled relationship. An inherent problem with living abroad is the stress caused by living in a new environment and the additional stress of confronting a foreign language and culture. A marriage or partnership that is in trouble, or a family with strained relationships, is more likely to crumble with the added pressure. Couples and families who start out with healthy relationships often find that their ties are strengthened by an international assignment. Each person is able to offer the support and encouragement necessary to create a positive environment with open lines of communication.

- **How much do you know about daily life in the country you are moving to?** It's one thing to know about the history of a country, to be familiar with the cultural icons, and know where the best hotels are. But how much do you know about the infrastructure of the country? How much does it cost to live there? What is it like to go shopping? What is the definition of "service" in that country? Will you be able to find the foods you like, go to a nightclub alone, ski? In other words, will you be able to find all of the things that you count on to make your life easier and more pleasurable? And if you can't, can you live without them or find acceptable substitutes? These are very important questions to answer before you go. Most of the information is not difficult to find if you are willing to look for it. You can use the Internet, find books, or talk to people who have lived there.

Of course, you may not be planning this relocation alone, and, if not, there's a good deal to consider regarding your children and your partner. We'll start with the children.

IMPACT ON CHILDREN

Accepting an international assignment is a decision that affects everyone in your family, including children. Kids react in a variety of ways, including excitement, resentment, and fear. Children can benefit enormously from living internationally. They develop the ability to look at the world multi-dimensionally and the ability to interact successfully with a wide variety of people; they also tend to be open-minded and less judgmental. Unfortunately, at the beginning of an assignment, those benefits are on a distant horizon. What you have to deal with immediately is getting your children acclimated to their new lives as painlessly as possible.

Any kind of move can be difficult for children; being uprooted from friends and school and getting adjusted to a strange place is not easy. With an international move and the usual questions of "Will anyone like me?" and "Will I be able to make friends?", children have to deal with a new culture where kids may look different, talk differently, or act differently—or all of the above. Fortunately, there are many steps you can take to smooth the transition.

First of all, involve children in the decision to move abroad. That is not to say that you must allow your child the chance to veto the move. The first reaction of most children to any move—domestic or international—is generally negative. (In fact, if a child reacts positively, it may be a sign of an underlying problem. Your child may be viewing the move an escape hatch.) But you can let your child know as early as possible about the move. Take the time to discuss why the move is necessary. This is especially important for older children and teens. They are old enough to be involved in discussions about why this move will help Mom's or Dad's career.

Secondly, let your child express all of his feelings about the move. A child's emotions will probably run the gamut from anger to excitement at one time or another. Share your own feelings, too. Let your child know that it's a little scary for you, too, but also exciting. Most importantly, let your child know that it's okay to feel anxious, excited, scared or angry.

Another important way to help children adjust is to talk about expectations. Be optimistic, but prepare to accept the bad as well as the good. Don't hide the fact that it is going to be hard at times, but don't forget to emphasize the positive. Help your kids learn about their destination. Make it a family project in which you all participate. The more realistic your child's expectations are—and your own too, incidentally—the easier the transition will be.

An easy way to ease a transition abroad is to take items from the house and from your child's room that will make the new house or apartment feel like home. Continuity is a key factor in a child's adjustment. Even though it may be tempting to leave a lot of items and replace them when you get to your destination, try to take as many of your children's belongings as possible. It is worth the trouble of packing and shipping if your child's bicycle or her own familiar bed will help her become comfortable with her new home.

Just as you involved your children in the decision to move, involve children in the actual move as much as possible. Children feel helpless during an international move. They are being moved abroad without having much say in the matter. It will help lessen the feelings of helplessness if you let children make as many decisions as you can. Let your child choose favorite toys or furniture, a favorite picture from the living room, or other items that you will take with you.

Allow your children the opportunity to say goodbye to their

friends. Have a party and let the children invite their friends, or enlist the help of a teacher in throwing a class party. Take videos or lots of pictures to make an album to take with you. Adults are sometimes surprised that young children have as deep an attachment to their playmates and possessions as older children. With all children, it is important to recognize the sense of loss and grieving that children go through when moving. Making "good good-byes" is an important step in being ready to accept the new.

Finally, make plans for staying in touch with family and friends. Make an address book for younger children to write down the addresses of their friends so that they can write. Think about other ways to stay in touch, such as writing a round-robin newsletter, faxing, e-mailing, or creating an audio- or videotape that you can send home. Create a schedule for making weekly or monthly telephone calls, writing letters, or making your tapes.

There is no formula that you can use to determine how your child is going to react. And obviously two children in the same family can have totally opposite reactions, with one skipping cheerfully off to school right away and one suffering stomachaches which double him over in pain. Personality plays a part in the adjustment, but so do the parents and the environment created in the new home. Following are some descriptions of general behavior patterns. As you read these descriptions, consider how your child has reacted to stressful situations in the past; this will give you insight into how she might react to an international move—which is most assuredly stressful—and give some thought to how you can help her manage her cultural transition.

Infants and Toddlers

While the biggest disruption for infants is the change in sleeping and eating schedules, toddlers will have a harder time understanding what is happening and will require a great deal of reassurance, before, during, and after the move. Distress at this age often results in a regression to babyish, clinging behavior.

Preschoolers

Preschool-aged children should be involved in the move as much as possible. Create ways that they can help, such as selecting which toys and clothing to bring and which to leave, labeling the boxes from his or her room, and packing for the trip. Seeing things being put into boxes and knowing that they will be unpacked in a few weeks is reassuring. Games will help explain the move; you can stage a play move with a dollhouse or by packing up and "moving" in your child's wagon. Coloring and activity books and picture books of your destination will add to the sense of security. Don't forget that shipped boxes may take several weeks to arrive. Make sure you take some of your familiar items on the plane with you.

Preteens

Older children will have more questions and will require more explanations. Take the time to discuss why you are moving, and be open about your feelings about moving. It helps children to know that their parents are sad to be leaving behind the people they know but are looking forward to a new experience. Learn with your children about your new country. Make trips to the library and select books that you can read together. Get a world map and a map of the country so they can see where they are going. Work with your children's teachers to make a presentation about the country. Learn about the food, traditional clothing, or holidays of the country. You can also help your children learn some phrases in the new language. Make a game of learning how to say "please" and "thank you" and other simple phrases. And give older children as much responsibility as possible in getting ready to move.

Teens

Teenagers often have the most difficulty with a major move. They are at a time in their lives when they are trying to establish an identity separate from their families and gain independence. The identity

being shaped is linked to friends and social activities; changes make
things all the more difficult. Moving to another country adds more
pressure in the form of a potential language barrier and unknown
customs. The best way to help teenagers through this period is
through open communication. Let them know that what they are
feeling is okay. You can also help by finding out as much information
as possible about where you are going. Get information on the new
school, including the curriculum and extracurricular activities. Finding out how kids dress and what they like to do when they get together is important too.

Although living abroad is a rewarding experience, some circumstances make it preferable to allow a teenager to remain behind for
the remainder of a semester or a school year (especially for students
in their last year of school). Include your teenager in the discussion
and make the decision based on the needs of your family.

All children, no matter what age, pick up on and, to a certain extent, reflect the behavior of their parents. Therefore, a positive attitude on your part is the best way to influence your children. Your
enthusiasm and acceptance of your new life will help them adjust; the
way you handle your own frustrations will set the example for them.

IMPACT ON SPOUSES OR PARTNERS

In the majority of cases, expatriates who accompany their spouse or
partner abroad are not able to get the necessary permit to work in the
host country. If you are giving up or postponing a career or job to
make this move with your partner, you are suddenly faced with a great
deal of free time that you will have to occupy in the new country.

Giving Up or Postponing a Career

At first glance, having several months—or even several years—of
free time may sound like a dream come true. In fact, there are probably few people who wouldn't welcome an extended vacation. However, you will find that after a couple of weeks of inactivity, you will

begin to feel restless. For most people who work, a career provides a lot of their self-identity and a feeling of self-worth, and its absence will certainly leave a void.

Being a Stay-at-Home Parent

When there are children in the family, the accompanying partner often decides to give up his or her career with the expectation that staying at home with the kids will provide more than enough to do. Before making this decision, here are a couple of issues to consider.

- How old are your children?
- Will your children be attending school?
- If your children will be in school, how do you plan to occupy your time when they are gone?
- Are there ways to get involved with your children's activities (i.e., volunteering at the school, coaching, leading field trips, etc.)?

DUELING CAREERS

The most pressing concern for dual-career couples is usually finding a position for the accompanying partner. It is important to stress that, while it is not always possible to find a paid position, there are usually plenty of other opportunities. The best way to find a "job" while you are living abroad is to redefine what "work" is. Broaden your definition from a nine-to-five job to include a host of other things, such as volunteering (which may lead to a paid position), freelancing, consulting, continuing your education, or learning new skills.

The following questions will help you begin to plan for identifying an occupation while you are abroad.

- Is it possible to get the permit you need to be eligible to work in that country? Can your company or your partner's company help you obtain one?

- Are there any opportunities within your company in the new location (either in a local office, if there is one, or as a consultant or working on a project for your company that can be accomplished from abroad)?
- Are there any similar opportunities within your partner's company?
- Are there entrepreneurial possibilities that you can pursue while abroad?
- Does either your company or your partner's company offer any type of career counseling or job-location assistance that would help you find a suitable position abroad? (This can sometimes be negotiated as part of the relocation package.)
- Are there volunteer opportunities in your field that you would consider appropriate substitutes for a paid position?
- Are there other opportunities outside of your field that you would consider appropriate substitutes for a paid position?
- Do you have a hobby or other interest that you could capitalize on? For example, if you have an interest in photography, can you freelance or assist a professional photographer?
- Is this an opportunity to make a career change? You will have a period of time that you can put to use learning new skills or developing your skills in a different direction.

So far in this section we've taken a look at some important points to remember when considering the impact of a move abroad on yourself, your children, and your partner. Another major issue is cultural adaptation, or, in other words, what you should expect as you look ahead at your and your family's acclimation to a new culture.

UNDERSTANDING CULTURAL ADAPTATION

Culture shock, or cultural disorientation, is the result of finding yourself in a culture that is new and unfamiliar. People in the new culture not only speak a different language, they also live by a different set of rules, with different values, attitudes, and behaviors. In some cases, these differences are immediately obvious; in others they are quite subtle. Cultural disorientation results in a range of emotional reaction, from irritation and frustration to anxiety and insecurity to resentment and anger. If the cultural adaptation process is not well managed, it will lead to depression.

No one is immune to culture shock; even frequent travelers and people who have lived abroad before feel its effect. The exception to the rule is the person who experiences mild culture shock in an abbreviated form. For the vast majority of sojourners, culture shock has a significant impact. The key to managing the cultural adaptation process is understanding what it is and developing an awareness of how it is affecting you personally. Once you reach this understanding, you will be ready to take steps to manage the stress caused by culture shock.

Culture shock is an emotional cycle with four distinct periods: enchantment, disenchantment, retreat, and adjustment. Although most people experience all four periods, each person's cycle is different; even different members of the same family will go through the ups and downs at different times.

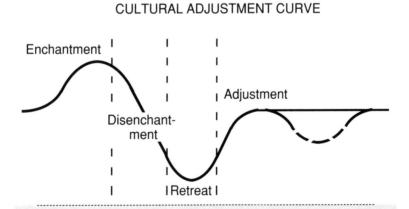

CULTURAL ADJUSTMENT CURVE

Enchantment

Disenchant-
ment

Adjustment

Retreat

Enchantment

Your arrival in your new home is an exciting time. Your senses are operating at top speed as you try to assimilate all of the new sights, sounds, and smells. You want to see and do everything. There are many new things to learn and discoveries to make. The differences that you notice between your home country and your new country are charming.

Disenchantment

After several weeks, a period of disenchantment typically sets in. As you establish your routine in your new country, reality begins to intrude on your enchantment. You have to deal with the mail carrier, the plumber, and your neighbors. Even simple tasks become difficult. When you go shopping, you may not recognize the food, and you may not be able to find what you want and what you're used to. People may seem rude, overly friendly, or just plain different. It is emotionally taxing to speak a new language, to use a new currency, and to perform all of the other minor details that you never gave a second thought to at home. With the new reality comes a sense of frustration and irritation, and often insecurity, since all of the cues you never had to think about before have changed.

Retreat

As you begin to feel more and more frustrated, tension and resentment will begin to build up. The retreat stage of the adjustment cycle is the most difficult. It becomes harder to leave your home. If you work, you may find yourself working late or coming straight home from the office. You turn down invitations and minimize contact with the culture and people in the new country. What was once "charming" or "interesting" about the country and customs has become "strange" and "stupid." In the constant comparison between your home country and the host country, home wins hands down. Homesickness is acute.

Adjustment

Finally, you will have to make the effort to adjust, to reestablish contact with the world and go on with your life. Your attitude will determine how you reconcile yourself to the things that are different in your new country. The people who make the most successful adjustments are those who realize that there are things that you like and dislike in any culture; doubtless there are things that you didn't care for at home, too. If you are willing to accept the culture, enjoy the things that you love about the culture, and find ways to accommodate the parts that you do not like, you will be happy. Once you have managed a successful adaptation, you will realize that you have gained a new set of skills, and are able to operate effectively within a new culture.

. . . and Beyond

If you take another look at the Cultural Adjustment Curve, you will notice a second dip. Many people experience a second low period, or even a series of ups and downs. Just when you think you've finally got things figured out, you stumble again. Subsequent periods of disillusionment might be more or less severe than the first; both reactions are normal.

KEYS TO A SUCCESSFUL ADJUSTMENT

The keys to a successful adjustment are self-awareness and acceptance. In order to be able to recognize cultural differences and effectively deal with them, you must first be aware of your own cultural values and attitudes.

Acceptance, the second key, means understanding that the culture, customs and rules in your new country, however far from your home country, are valid. Once you are able to accept them as different, rather than better or worse than your own, you will be more comfortable and able to adapt to new ways of doing things.

Understand that the ups and downs of cultural adjustment are normal; everyone who has moved before you has experienced the same process, complete with similar symptoms. If you reach out to those people, they can help you through the process. They will tell you that they survived and so will you.

Even after you have adjusted, you will have good days, when you feel at ease in your new culture, and bad days, when you question your sanity in deciding to move there. Once you have completely adjusted, the good days will eclipse the bad.

Coping Techniques

The psychological disorientation of an international move causes a tremendous amount of stress. In order to manage your cultural adaptation successfully, you must find an outlet for this stress. Think for a moment about how you relieve stress in your life right now. Stress outlets can be physical, such as jogging or biking, or mental, such as meditation or reading. List your stress relievers on a piece of paper. Once you've made your list, think about how you can continue those activities in your new home. Some of them—meditation, for instance—are easily transported. Some, however, may require modification or planning. For example, if you're used to riding your bike through the country lanes near your home but you will be moving to a crowded urban center, you may have to modify your activity. Can you use a stationary bike instead? Are there nearby parks or other areas where you can safely bike?

If you are not sure about the availability of a specific activity, make it a priority to find out. There are many resources, including other expatriates, people from your new country who may live in your area, consulates, books, and more.

FAMILIES

Families who have relocated to another country move with their own built-in support network to help each member through the process of adaptation. However, relocation also often means that family roles shift. A spouse who was a breadwinner before moving abroad might become a dependent; normally independent children may find themselves dependent on their parents, at least initially.

An international assignment often includes regional responsibilities that require frequent travel or extended business trips. If one partner is required to travel often, the other is left taking on more of the shared responsibilities in order to fill the gap left by the numerous absences. At times one feels like a single parent, even if it's not the case! Of course, the partner who is frequently away can find himself or herself feeling left out of the family upon returning.

All of these changes can be successfully managed if you have open lines of communication. Parents will benefit by talking with each other about the changes that are necessary to accommodate the new situation and by discussing ways that they can support each other to maintain consistency. The whole family will function better if everyone feels comfortable expressing fears and concerns and receives encouragement and support from other family members.

THE NON-WORKING PARTNER

Unlike children and the working partner, a non-working partner faces a new life that is without the inherent structure of school or work. So once the initial settling in is done, your partner goes to work every day, and the children traipse off to school, you are left with nothing to do. If you were used to working, this is especially difficult. Even if you were not employed prior to the move, you still have left behind all of the familiar routines that filled your day.

According to article after article, many unsuccessful assignments are attributed to a non-working partner who is unhappy in the new culture. This puts a lot of pressure on you; but with some effort and planning, you can put that particular worry aside.

In the absence of outside activities, the world of a non-working partner is limited to household chores and the lives of children and the spouse. In the initial months, these same children and spouses have spent the majority of the day coping with their own stresses in the new culture and are rarely in the mood for scintillating conversation when they return to the sanctuary of home.

The more activities that you are involved in, the more fulfilled your own life will be. These activities can include your family, such as volunteering at your child's school, or they can be a pursuit of your own interests. The possibilities are practically endless. Other than volunteering, you can use the spare time to take classes, develop new skills, or pursue a hobby. If you give your imagination free rein, there are plenty of things that you can do. See the dual career sections throughout the book for other ideas on making the most of your time abroad.

CHILDREN

Children go through their own adjustment process, just as adults do. Younger children often feel frightened in a new location where everything is different from what they are used to: the people may look different, buildings may look different, and things certainly sound and smell different. Sometimes children (and adults, too) become an object of curiosity if they are living in a country where they look greatly different from the locals (for example, an American child in a small Japanese town). They are often uncomfortable being stared at and even touched by curious strangers. Younger children will have difficulty understanding what the move means and may tend to relate the move to vacations that they have experienced. They may be waiting for the trip to be over and for the family to return to their familiar surroundings at home. When the return home does not happen, they can get very upset. This may not happen for several weeks, or even months, so that a child who seems to have adjusted just fine might have problems down the road. Symptoms of their distress may be quite physical, such as stomachaches, or emotional, such as withdrawal and depression.

Older children, who do understand the implication of an international move and who realize that this move is not permanent, may be reluctant to get too deeply involved with friends, trying to protect themselves from the pain of making friends only to leave again after a year or two.

Throughout the process of adjustment, children will experience periods of anger. This is understandable since they have been dragged across the world against their wishes. It is important to allow children, whatever their age, to express their anger and to provide appropriate outlets for it.

Keep in mind, too, that younger children may not be able to put their feelings into words. You can help them express their feelings by taking along children's books about moving that will help them find the words to tell you what is wrong.

Naturally, all children will react differently to an international move. The best way to cope is with patience and understanding.

Global Nomads and Third-Culture Kids

Global nomads, also called Third-Culture Kids, are people who have lived overseas before adulthood, usually because of a parent's job. The global nomad is abroad without choice; the parents have chosen an international lifestyle, usually with the expectation that they will eventually return to the passport country. When children live abroad for a long period of time—or even for fairly short periods of time— they become culturally different from the parents. Their whole avenue of cultural exploration is very different from that of one born and reared in one place (as the parents often are).

Living internationally is a unique opportunity for children. It is a heritage that will shape the rest of their lives. While overseas, children develop a whole host of global skills, including multilingual skills, the ability to view situations from two different sides, and mediating and cross-cultural skills—simply by living. It is a heritage that can be applied very usefully in today's global arena.

One of the biggest challenges of moving abroad is to maintain the cultural identity of children. Children are absorbing the new culture through school, caregivers, and what they observe in the world around them. "Home" becomes a place to go on vacation once or twice a year. Parents can keep children connected to their own culture in a variety of ways, such as observing the holidays and traditions of their home culture. It is also helpful to keep in contact with what's going on at home, both with friends and family members and through magazines and newspapers.

PARENTING ABROAD

Raising a child abroad is an added challenge. Depending on where you are living, the values may be different than those you want to instill in your children. Children learn not only from their parents, but from school, peers, other caregivers, and society in general. Imagine that you have told your teenagers that they must be a certain age before they can drink, but they are suddenly confronted with vending machines in Japan that sell whiskey with no restrictions. This doesn't mean that Japan has a rampant problem with teenage alcoholism; it simply indicates that Japanese children are governed by different societal and parental restraints than your child. These kinds of problems are best dealt with by establishing very clear family rules. Have family meetings to establish and reinforce the rules.

A lack of organized activities for teenagers is often a problem. You and your child may have to actively search for the activities he or she likes to do. If you can't find appropriate activities, think about organizing a baseball team, a drama group, or other activities yourself. Encourage your children to bring their friends over, and try to meet their friends' parents, just as you would at home.

In some countries, the expatriate life itself can pose hazards in the form of making children accustomed to a higher standard of living than most people. Some people find themselves in a position to obtain household help. If you have never had this experience, it will take some time to be comfortable having someone work for you. You may have to train the people you hire, and you should definitely be clear on your expectations; do not assume, for example, that your idea of disciplining your children is shared by the person you hire to baby-sit your child.

If you are lucky enough to have household help, you may find that your children come to expect that someone will pick up after them and believe that they are not personally responsible for any chores. If that is contrary to what you want your children to learn, you may want to continue to assign some household tasks to children to reinforce your own values to them.

DUAL-CAREER COUPLES

Dual-career couples with children face the same issues as other families, but with an additional concern: child care. You are leaving behind your own child care network and will have to rebuild it from scratch. This can be complicated, especially if your extended family plays a major role in child care or in countries where public or private child care is rare. Even if your children are in school, there may not be structured activities for them to participate in during the time between school and the end of the workday. There are options if you search for them. Think about the following ideas:

- Hire an au pair, nanny, or other live-in help
- Look for formal or informal networks within the expat community; often there is a system of sharing child care
- If your job has the flexibility, work at home or part-time
- Approach a neighbor or another family about looking after your child during the day
- Find an older person who would be interested in caring for your child (this has the added benefit of providing your child with a "grandparent")

If you are not able to find viable child care options, you may be able to create something that will meet your needs. And there are sure to be other families who would welcome the alternative. Don't rule out starting a day care center for younger children or organizing after-school activities for older children.

The most important thing, of course, is that you feel comfortable with your child care arrangements and that you trust the person who will be caring for your children.

THE SINGLE LIFE

Living abroad as a single person has both ups and downs. Moving to a place where you have no network of friends is difficult; coping with a new country and culture where you may not know how to go about meeting people to create your new social network is even tougher. In many countries, a person's work and home lives are kept quite separate. Social bonds have been formed throughout the years in school and elsewhere; business relationships do not necessarily translate into social relationships. And, in many cases, the family and extended family play a significant role in a person's life, and a great deal of time is spent in family activities. All of this can make it seem impossible for a newly arrived person to meet people and form friendships.

On the other hand, expatriates are often not subject to the same 'rules' as everyone else. Most expatriates find people in their host country to be very sympathetic to their situation, interested in learning more about them, and open to the possibilities of a relationship that extends beyond office hours. With luck, you will find yourself the recipient of invitations from your colleagues.

In the final analysis, though, it is up to you to build your new life. There are many avenues open to you. The best way to meet people, in fact, is to simply do something that you like to do. If you like to hike, go hiking; if you like to work out, join a gym. By doing something that interests you, you are putting yourself into situations where you can meet people with the same interests.

Another possibility to explore is the expatriate community. Where there are significant numbers of expatriates, there are usually networks in place, both for business and social purposes. Often there is a newcomer's club that provides activities and events for socializing. In these organizations, too, you will find people who have gone through the relocation and adaptation process and who have firsthand knowledge of what you are experiencing. These can be invaluable contacts throughout your own process of adaptation, giving you the support and encouragement you need, or even a shoulder to cry on when necessary.

Singles often have a unique experience abroad. Because they are not accompanied by a family, they generally have much more contact with the language and culture of the host country. An expatriate with a family goes home at the end of the day, speaks his or her native tongue at home, and is shielded from the language and culture to some extent. A single person does not have that shield, and spends more time speaking the new language and immersed in the culture through his or her social life. That person often has the added benefit of learning the language more quickly and thoroughly and of adapting to the new culture quickly.

THE GENDER FACTOR

The myth that women are not able to be successful in some cultures has largely been debunked. Instead, many experts say that, in fact, women are often better equipped to be successful than men. Most women find that they are viewed first and foremost as foreigners and are therefore not subject to all of the rules that apply to the local women. So even in cultures where women are not traditionally found in business, the same barriers do not apply to foreign women. In fact, many women have found that they can use the curiosity of local businessmen to their advantage and get their foot in the door more easily than their male counterparts. One issue that women do face, on a very personal level, is whether or not they can accept the local culture—specifically the role and treatment of women. This does not mean that you have to behave exactly like the local women (although there may be certain amount of conformation required of you), but you do have to be able to live with what is happening around you. This is a very personal decision; if you are uncomfortable with a culture's general attitude toward women, then perhaps it is better to wait for another assignment in a country where you feel more comfortable. Take care, though, that you understand the values that underlie the explicit behavior; it is easy to confuse the desire to protect with the desire to restrict.

THE RACE FACTOR

Most people of color find that they are seen first as being American, or Canadian, or British, etc. In countries where there is a history of discrimination against a certain minority group, usually an immigrant group, those rules simply do not apply to expatriates. There is no general formula for the experience that people of color have internationally. As in the case of one African-American, some expatriates feel that they actually have an advantage because they are used to being in the minority, which can make the adjustment to the new culture easier than for someone who is used to being part of the majority. As with the gender issue, it is not a question of the situation being good or bad; the issue is how you personally handle being in the limelight. In another case, a woman of Puerto Rican descent who grew up in New York considered herself to be an American and not a minority, with little thought of her cultural roots. When she was given an assignment in Latin America, she began to explore the Latino culture and began to value that part of her heritage.

There are cases, however, where people of color do encounter difficulty. This occurs most often when a person relocates to his or her ancestral home. For example, a Japanese-American might be selected for an international assignment in Japan. Usually the selection is made because of the "Japanese" part of the equation, with little thought of the "American" part. In other words, the selection is made because someone looks the part. This strategy can backfire, though. Even if that person speaks Japanese, he has absorbed the American culture and holds many American values since that is where he spent his formative years. The difficulty arises because he looks Japanese, but does not act Japanese. The result can be suspicion, distrust, or ostracism on the part of the Japanese. Similar situations confront many Asian-Americans whose families immigrated generations ago, including "overseas Chinese," and Vietnamese-Americans. These issues can be minimized or avoided if you have an awareness of who you are and an understanding of the culture that you will be living in, especially the ways in which it is different from your own blended culture.

SEXUAL ORIENTATION

If you are lesbian or gay, you will probably want to do some research on the acceptance of homosexuals in the country you will be living in before you embark on your international assignment. While some countries have laws preventing discrimination against anyone because of sexual orientation, the acceptance of homosexuals by the society in general ranges from tolerance to homophobia. Make sure you are also aware of any laws prohibiting homosexual acts, and the possible consequences of practicing your sexuality. These concerns will affect bisexuals and transgendered people as well.

Moving abroad with a same-sex partner presents certain challenges not faced by married partners, as it is virtually impossible for an accompanying partner to get a work visa without being legally married. In addition, few companies include same-sex partners in the expatriate benefit package, causing complications in matters such as housing allowances, insurance, and allowances for the loss of the partner's income. As an accompanying partner, you must focus on the alternatives that are available to you in the new country. Issues of giving up or postponing a career must be dealt with, and work alternatives must be investigated. Be proactive in exploring your options. Try to talk to people who have experience living in the country, both natives of the country and expatriates who have lived there. The more people you can talk to, the more complete a picture you will have about the implications of being lesbian, gay, bisexual, or transgendered in your new culture.

A WORD ABOUT "EXPATRIATE CLUBS"

Many expatriates are wary of expatriate clubs, seeing them as a group of spouses who get together to play tennis and bridge. Even if there are people in the organization who do play bridge, the clubs are much more than that. Expatriate organizations are an excellent source of information on everyday issues, such as for finding a doctor; for networking, which accompanying partners who are seeking jobs or alternatives can tap into; for learning about the culture through structured activities and events; and for socializing. Each individual can decide how much he or she wants to be involved in the expatriate community. Indeed, there are plenty of expatriates who immerse themselves in it, and have very little contact with local-country nationals. There are also people who avoid it altogether. You are free to choose either, or any point in the spectrum between. Just keep in mind that the expatriate network can be invaluable; it can also provide that touch of home when you need it.

STAYING IN TOUCH

Even if you are excited about the prospect of living abroad, don't forget to make plans to stay in touch. You will want to hear from your family and friends at home, and keep them up-to-date on your own adventures. It's very easy to get swept up in your new life, and difficult to find the time to write or call with all of the new challenges of living abroad. However, the people who form your network of support will continue to be important as you adjust to your life abroad, especially during difficult times.

Establishing and maintaining a systematic way of communicating with home is also critical when it comes time to return after your sojourn abroad—something that is difficult to think about when you haven't even left yet!

ROUND TRIP TICKET: THE RETURN HOME

Contrary to what you might think, the return home, or repatriation, after an international assignment is often a more difficult transition than moving abroad.

Professional Repatriation

One of the hazards of living and working internationally is that when you return, you can find yourself out of touch with your home office and with changes in your field or profession. Without proper preparation, you may find yourself without an office, without direction, and, indeed, without a job. Many former expatriates have returned to the home country after a successful assignment, only to have to wait for a suitable position to open up. In addition, many returned expatriates find that their experience abroad and newly acquired skills and knowledge are not put to use by the organization. A marketing manager fresh from an assignment in Asia may find herself in a domestic marketing position with little or no involvement in any global markets. Even if the goal of the assignment was your professional development with an eye toward "globalization" or developing the international market, it is difficult to put those lofty goals to work practically. It is up to you to ensure that you are receiving the support you need during the assignment and to plan your strategy for reintegration into the home or local office.

If you moved abroad with your partner but were unable to work abroad, you face some of the same challenges when you return. You may feel that technology has passed you by, or that the skills you used before you moved are rusty from disuse. The best way to counteract this is to think about coming home while you are abroad and make sure that you keep your skills up to date—and maybe even develop new skills or expertise!

Following these steps can ease your professional reentry:

- Set a strategy before you go. Getting the support of upper management is crucial. Make sure you have a clear understanding of the objective of sending you abroad, what your goals are during the assignment, and exactly how you will fit back into the organization when you return.

- Stay in touch while you are abroad. In the case of international assignees, "out of sight, out of mind" holds true more often than not. Remind the home office of all of the points outlined above. Keep them informed about what you are doing and your accomplishments. And keep yourself informed about what is going on at the home office, promotions and staff changes, important policy changes, etc. E-mail and faxes are readily available in most companies; take advantage of technology to maintain contact.

• Find a mentor. In fact, find two or three. Mentors will help keep you in the minds of the decision- and policy-makers and keep you informed about what's going on at home. Mentoring relationships do not have to be formalized. And by finding several mentors, you won't find yourself returning from your assignment only to find that your champion in the company no longer works there!

• Visit the home office whenever you can. While you are on a home leave or business trip back, take the opportunity to reconnect with colleagues. Make use of the time to familiarize yourself with recent changes.

Even if you take all of the recommended steps to stay in touch, understand that things will be different when you return. The fact is, the company and your colleagues have grown in the time you have been away, just as you have. It will take time and patience to reintegrate yourself into the new environment.

Personal Repatriation

Personal repatriation can also be painful. During your sojourn, you will have gained new insights and new perspectives. You will realize that there is really no right or wrong way to do things, only different ways. In addition, most people remember "home" with fondness while they are away, forgetting about the things that aren't so great. And, of course, you will come home to find that your home country has its share of blemishes, just like everywhere else. This means that you will go through another cycle of adjustment as you refamiliarize yourself with your home culture and come to terms with the bad as well as the good in it.

If you are gone for several years, you will experience some disorientation when you return. Things will have changed, and you will have had a long period of time that you have not shared experiences with your family and friends. You may find some people who aren't interested in hearing about your experiences abroad, or who roll their eyes when you say "When I was in . . . ." You may even encounter people who feel that you are putting on airs or that you feel superior because of your experience. You will have to come to terms with the fact that the people you knew before you left have changed, as you have, but in different ways.

There are ways to ease your personal readjustment.

- Stay in touch while you are gone. This can be difficult as you immerse yourself in your new life. Just as you fade from prominence at home, home fades for you. You will have to make a conscious effort to maintain regular contact, and make sure your kids do. The benefit of doing this is that when you return, there is less of a void in your experiences; you have kept people informed of important events in your lives, and vice versa.

- Visit home whenever possible. This is especially important if you have children. As well as helping you keep in contact with friends and family, it helps children maintain their sense of "home" and their cultural identity.

- Realize that your return home will have its ups and downs, just as your adjustment to living abroad did.

Children's Repatriation

The most difficult part of readjustment for children is that they have a gap in their lives where they have missed all of the pieces of popular culture that their friends have experienced, such as music, movies, TV, toys, and the way kids dress. They have to learn the current slang, and how kids talk. Along with this, they are different from their peers. They have developed in ways that kids at home have not, and they have a different frame of reference. More than adults, children who return home after living abroad will find that their peers see them as thinking that they are superior and resent references to "When I was in . . . ."

Tips for Staying in Touch

Most of us are accustomed to picking up the telephone and calling someone whenever we want. If you are living in another country, though, you may find that this isn't as easy any more because of time difference, poor international phone service, or the prohibitive cost of international calls. Here are some suggestions for alternative ways of staying in touch.

- **The old standby: write letters**. Since the advent of the telephone, most of us are no longer letter-writers. When phoning is too expensive, this is one of the cheapest alternatives. However, it's also the slowest!

- **Fax letters**. Write your letter, then fax it. This will give you the satisfaction of instantaneous communication, without the prohibitive cost of an extended telephone call. Family and friends without a fax machine may be able to arrange to receive faxes at work or elsewhere.

- **E-mail**. Probably the least expensive alternative, although not an alternative in all locations.

- **Chatting online.** If you and your family/friends all have Internet access, and you are able to access the Internet from your new country, try scheduling a time to find a quiet corner to chat online. Some of the larger services such as CompuServe and AOL offer service in many countries. Just remember that you

may have to pay for local connect time rates—check with your
service provider.

- **Use the company's phone**. With the company's permission, of
course! As part of the expatriate package, some companies will
allow you and your family members limited use of office
phones to make international calls.

- **Videotapes or cassettes**. Although it will take a while to get
there, videotapes and cassettes are more personal than writing
letters. It's especially nice if you have children. You can exchange tapes with family members, and your children can exchange them with friends and even their classes at school. Be
sure you will have access to the right equipment, since many
countries use PAL instead of VHS. A further word of caution:
be careful not to run afoul of the local laws. For example, in
some countries, a videotape that includes your sister frolicking
on the beach in a bikini may be considered pornography locally,
even if you don't think it is. Make sure you know all of the applicable laws.

- **Write a newsletter**. This is especially helpful if you've got a long
list of people you want to keep in contact with. Document what
is happening in your life, write about the funny things that happen, about current events in your new community, or anything
else that appeals. Or start a round-robin letter, where everyone
who receives the letter adds to the letter and passes it on to the
next person.

- **Schedule regular phone calls**. It's bad enough to reach an an-
swering machine when you want to talk to someone. It's worse
when you are paying international rates to talk to a machine! If
you talk to someone often, try to arrange for a regular time to
call—every Sunday night at 10:00, the last Saturday of each
month, or whatever fits both of your schedules.

LEARNING ABOUT YOUR NEW HOME

You're on your way to a new adventure. Now is the time to gather all of the information you need to make your international sojourn successful. Learning the language (if it's different from yours) and learning about the culture of your new home should be prioritized.

Learning the language of the country you will be living in is an obvious necessity. The more you learn of the language, the more you will feel at home. If it happens to be a language you already speak, great; if not, get started as soon as possible. Make it your goal to learn at least basic phrases before you go, more if possible. This book comes complete with a special language section and an audio CD for just that. While some people have a facility for learning languages, others find it more difficult. And it is often more difficult for adults than for children. Yes, you will make mistakes, and even embarrass yourself. It will be frustrating to have to struggle to express yourself, and you will feel awkward speaking with a limited vocabulary as you start out, but the effort is well worth it. The fact that you are willing to make the effort to adjust yourself to a new language will open many doors for you, and you will find that most people respond with delight. Learning the language also gives you the opportunity to really experience life in the local community in ways that are not possible if you are isolated from interaction by not speaking the local language.

Just as important as learning the language of your new country is learning about its culture and peoples. What are the values that the people hold? What is their history? What are their beliefs, customs, and traditions? In the Background chapter of this book, we've provided you with enough of this kind of information to whet your appetite. Don't stop there, though! There are lots of ways to go about learning about the culture of your new country, including reading books and articles, talking to other expatriates or people from the country, and participating in a pre-departure (or post-arrival!) cultural orientation. Don't expect to learn everything there is to learn about the country in such a short time, or imagine that you will be prepared for every contingency; your goal is to learn enough to be comfortable in your new home. Once you arrive, you will discover on your own much more than you can ever learn from a book or from talking to other people.

Perhaps the first step in learning about your new culture is to learn about yourself and your own culture. Because culture is such an innate part of who we are, few people take the time to ponder what it is that makes them tick. Spend some time reflecting on your own cultural heritage, and ask yourself the same questions you would ask of another culture: What are your values? What is your history? What are your beliefs, customs and traditions? The more you understand about yourself, the easier it will be for you to recognize cultural differences and reduce the likelihood of cultural misunderstandings.

MOVING ABROAD "DOS & DON'TS"

DO . . .

   . . . have realistic expectations.
   . . . find out as much as you can before you go.
   . . . learn the language—or at least basic phrases.
   . . . be open-minded.
   . . . find several mentors and cultural guides.
   . . . make plans now for keeping in touch.
   . . . take the initiative and reach out.

DON'T . . .

   . . . lose touch with family and friends.
   . . . wait until it is time to return to plan for your repatriation.
   . . . wait for other people to come to you.

FOUR

GETTING AROUND

GETTING AROUND LOCALLY

Whether you're visiting Japan for a short time or living there for an extended period, you have to be able to get from Point A to Point B. This chapter provides simple tips and practical information to help you get around locally and travel from city to city.

Driving

In Japan, the steering wheels are on the right side of the car and you'll be driving on the left side of the road. (So remember: wide right turns and narrow left turns.) Otherwise, however, the rules of the road are very similar to most Western countries and the symbols on signs are easily recognized. Many of the major roads have signs in English as well as Japanese, but traveling off the beaten path can be challenging if you don't read Japanese. If you would like a complete list of driving rules, you can purchase *Rules of the Road,* available in six languages, including English, from the Japanese Automobile Federation (JAF). This will be especially useful if you plan on applying for a Japanese driver's license.

Japan's expressway (*kousokudōro*) system is fairly limited and the tolls can add quite a bit of expense to your trip. You can, however, buy a prepaid toll card at tollbooths or service centers that will give you a small discount on tolls. You can purchase the toll card with a credit card. In fact, you can even use a major credit card to pay your toll when you reach the tollbooth.

Smaller national routes (*kokudō*) do not have tolls, but the speed limit is lower. Roads in rural areas are often narrow. Keep in mind, too, that much of Japan is mountainous, so driving can be quite a challenge for those not used to navigating mountain roads.

Parking in the city can be a hassle and it's usually not free. Free parking along the curb is virtually nonexistent, so expect to pay for a parking lot. If you are staying at a hotel, there may be free parking for guests, as with some restaurants and shops. If there is no on-site parking, you may be able to get parking validation for a nearby parking lot. Be sure you have your ticket with you, because you will probably need to get it stamped.

Driving Tips

- The speed limit on the expressway is 80 kilometers per hour (about 50 mph); on other roads the limit is usually 50 kilometers per hour (about 30 mph) and 40 kilometers per hour (about 25 mph) in cities.

- Gasoline prices are more expensive in Japan than in the U.S., but about comparable to European prices.

- Be cautious while driving in cities and towns; it's not uncommon for pedestrians to step onto the street without warning.

- Speed traps are common, especially in areas with low speed limits, since virtually everyone ignores them.

- Because finding a free legal parking space is next to impossible, many people park illegally at the curb. However, if your car is parked there for too long, it will be towed.

- If you see a green and yellow emblem in the shape of a downward-pointing chevron on the vehicle, it means that the driver has recently passed the driving test.

- JAF (Japanese Automobile Federation) is the Japanese equivalent of AAA (the American Automobile Association) and offers similar services, such as roadside assistance and travel discounts.

- Roadside emergency phones can be found alongside most major roads if your car breaks down or if you are in an accident. Note that road service on Japan's expressways was deregulated in 1997; if you are a member of JAF, you can ask for them when you use these phones in order to take advantage of your membership benefits.

- Drunk driving is taken very seriously in Japan and the laws were recently tightened and penalties stiffened. If you fail a breathalyzer test (0.25 is the limit, compared to 1 in the U.S.), you will lose your license immediately, incur a hefty fine, and possibly face a jail sentence of up to 15 years.

The streets of Japan's cities are usually overcrowded, so, generally speaking, it's more convenient to use the excellent public transportation system for local travel and save the driving for trips outside of the city.

Getting a Japanese
Driver's License

If you will be in Japan for less than six months, you will only need an International Driving Permit to supplement your national driving license. For longer sojourns, you will need to transfer your home license to a Japanese driver's license (a process called *gaimen kirikae*), which can be obtained from the Driver's License Center (*unten-menkyoshō*) in the precinct you live in. Note that in order to be eligible to switch to a Japanese license, you must have a valid license (you cannot transfer an expired license), and you must be able to prove that you lived in the country where your license was issued for at least three months after the issue date. If your home driver's license was issued less than three months before you arrive in Japan, you will have to attend driving school, which can cost up to 300,000 yen (¥), before you can get a Japanese driver's license.

Before going to the licensing center, you will need to have your home license translated into Japanese. This can be done at the Japanese Automobile Federation (JAF) or at foreign embassies and consulates. To have your license translated by JAF, take a photocopy of your license to a JAF office (see Appendix B for contact information) or mail it via registered mail. JAF currently charges ¥3,000 for the translation; if you submit your request by mail, there is an additional fee of ¥700 to cover the return postage.

Take the translation, your home driver's license, and your passport with you to the Driver's License Center, along with your resident card or alien registration card and one passport size photo (color or black-and-white). There is an application fee of ¥4,125 for the driver's license. You will take a simple eyesight and color blindness test, as well as a written and practical driving test. The multiple-choice written test is available in eight languages, including English. Licensed drivers from the UK, Australia, France, Germany, Sweden, Italy, and Spain are not required to take the practical driving test. Once you pass the tests, you will receive a Japanese license valid for two years following your next birthday.

Public Transportation

Getting around locally in Japan's major cities is easily and inexpensively accomplished using public transportation. If you are staying only a few days, or if you're visiting another city, look into purchasing a flat-rate day pass that will allow unlimited travel on the subway, trams, or bus, or an excursion pass that will let you travel on any combination of public transportation. Although these are not available everywhere, they can be found in several major cities, including Tokyo. If your stay extends a month or more, you can purchase booklets of discounted tickets (*kaisūken*) or commuter passes (*tsūkin teiki*).

Subways, Trams, and Trains

Many cities, including Tokyo and Osaka, have extensive subway or tram systems in addition to commuter trains to outlying areas. Subways and trams are state-run, but many of the trains to the suburbs are privately owned. Trains are slowly being phased out in most cities, since they contribute to traffic congestion problems.

You can buy your ticket at the ticket machine in the station or at the ticket counter. Most machines will accept coins or bills, and there is usually a change machine nearby if you only have large bills. Fares are based on the distance traveled, so check the rates for where you are going before putting your money in and selecting your destination. If you are unsure which fare to pay, simply choose the lowest fare and pay the difference to the ticket inspector when you arrive at your destination. If there is no one manning the exit gate, take the ticket to the fare adjustment office.

Some stations have manned entry gates while others are automatic. At automatic gates, simply insert your ticket into the slot and remove it when it is returned. If there is a ticket inspector, he or she will punch your ticket when you enter and collect it when you exit. Be sure you keep your ticket, since it will need to be checked when you exit as well.

If you're a casual traveler or if your schedule is flexible, try to avoid Japan's notorious rush hour (up until about 9:30 AM and after 4:00 PM in Tokyo) crunches. As everyone is rushing in to work and home at the end of the day, subways and trains are packed to several times their capacities. During these times, you will see *oshiya*, people whose job it is to push people into already packed cars so the doors can close.

Buses

Buses are certainly an option for traveling in cities, but they are, of course, subject to the vagaries of traffic. Unlike the trains, most local buses have a flat rate fare no matter what your destination is. Check at the bus station for information on routes and fares; you may also want to purchase *kaisūken*, or books of tickets at a discounted rate.

When you board, put your money in the fare box next to the driver; most accept either coins or notes, but change is given only for coins. Most buses have pre-recorded stop announcements, along with other miscellaneous announcements. When your stop is approaching, just press one of the buzzers mounted on the side of the bus. If you don't think you will recognize your stop, ask the driver to let you know when to get off the bus.

Tips for a Smooth Ride

Just a few minutes of observation would be enough to see that Americans and Japanese have different unwritten rules about riding in public transportation. Here are a few things to remember if you want to be a model passenger in Japan.

- Don't stare at other passengers. Many people close their eyes and rest during the trip.
- Keep your purse, briefcase, or anything else you may be carrying firmly at your side. Don't let it dangle and bump into other passengers.

- Don't take up more than one space. Many Americans, especially men, sit with their knees spread quite wide. Keep yourself as compact as possible to make room for everyone.
- There is no smoking allowed in trains, subways, or buses or on subway and train platforms.

Subways, trams, trains, and buses are safe, even at night. However, women traveling alone should be aware that there are some men who take advantage of crowded trains to touch or rub up against women. If this happens to you, you can make a loud verbal statement to draw attention to the man and shame him into leaving you alone, or you can push your way to another part of the train. The latter can be difficult at the height of rush hours, but other passengers will generally try to let you by if they realize what is going on. In an effort to prevent harassment, some trains have a separate "women-only" car, designated by a placard on the car.

Taxis

The first things that Americans notice about Japanese taxis is that the rear doors are operated automatically by the driver from inside the car. Unfortunately, this knowledge often comes at the price of a sharp smack on the wrist of the unsuspecting traveler who reaches for the door handle before it springs open automatically.

You can find taxi stands at hotels and train stations, or you can hail one in the street by raising your hand. All taxis have a sign on the roof and a light on the lower right corner of the windshield that indicates occupancy. When the light is lit up in red, it means the taxi is available. A green light signals an available taxi in the hours when the nighttime surcharge is in effect. It's best to avoid unlicensed taxis; you can distinguish registered taxis by their green license plates.

Passengers should ride in the back of the taxi unless there are too many people to fit. You can put your baggage in the trunk; there is no extra fee for luggage or parcels. All taxis have a meter that displays the fare. A surcharge is added between the hours of 11:00 PM and 5:00 AM. You will also pay a little extra if you have phoned for the taxi. It is not necessary to tip the taxi driver.

Taking a taxi can be quite challenging for the non-Japanese speaker in Japan for two reasons: most taxi drivers speak little to no English, and Japanese addresses are extremely confusing. (See the Living and Staying in Japan chapter for more information on addresses.) It's not enough to memorize or write down the address of your destination; unless you are going to a well-known place, such as a hotel or major business, you will probably also need to give directions to the driver. Therefore, it's a good idea to have someone write down both the address and directions whenever possible. If you don't have directions, don't be surprised if your taxi driver stops one or more times to ask for directions at a police kiosk or shop. Unless you know where you are going, finding a place with only an address to go on is akin to searching for buried treasure without the *X* conveniently marked on the map!

GETTING FROM CITY TO CITY

You have many options when it comes to getting from city to city, from driving to flying and everything in between.

Renting a Car

Renting a car in Japan is not difficult, as long as you have a major credit card and an International Driver's License, but it is expensive.

Rental offices tend to be most readily found near airports and train stations. You will find offices for several major international companies (such as Hertz and Dollar), national firms (such as Orix and Japaren), as well as local rental companies. The major automobile manufacturers, including Toyota, Mazda, Nissan, and Mitsubishi all have rental offices as well.

Round-trip rentals are a better deal than one-way trips, since most car rental companies tack on a surcharge for getting the car back to where it started, a cost that you must be prepared for if your destination is on a different island.

Be sure you check to see if your rental includes unlimited mileage; some companies charge after a certain number of kilometers.

Trains

Given the cost of car rentals and tolls and the congestion problems in large cities, train travel can be a more reliable and less stressful mode of travel. As an added bonus, Japan has an extensive network of trains crisscrossing the country and schedules are strictly adhered to, so you can rest assured that the 10:00 train will, in fact, arrive at 10:00.

Japanese trains come in several forms: *shinkansen,* or bullet trains, limited express and express trains, overnight trains, and local trains. The trains are all safe, clean, and comfortable.

Long distance service is provided by Japan Railway (JR), formerly Japan National Railway (JNR) before being privatized in 1986 and split into six regional rail companies. The six carriers operate in tandem, though, so the traveler will not even notice the seams in the service areas.

JR publishes a monthly book of timetables called the *JR Jikokuhyō* which lists the schedules of every imaginable form of intercity transportation, but you are likely to break your back carrying around this phonebook sized tome. As an alternative, you can buy the Japan Travel Bureau's (JTB) Mini-Timetable monthly publication, which lists most schedules for Tokyo, Osaka, and Nagoya and has the added benefit of some English explanations and names written in romaji, or Romanized characters.

Bullet Trains (Shinkansen)

Japan's bullet train, or *shinkansen,* is not only fast, it is convenient and safe as well. In more than thirty years of service there has not been one fatality on the bullet train. The *shinkansen* travel between Japan's major cities.

You will have to pay a supplement for a trip on a *shinkansen,* but you do not need a reservation, although you may end up standing in the aisle if the train is full.

There are three levels of service on the bullet train: the green car or first class, the regular reserved car or second class, and the non-

reserved car or third class; the latter class does not require reservations. If you're feeling peckish during your trip, you can usually find something to eat in the cafeteria car or buy a *ekiben* (boxed lunch) from the attendants who traverse the train's aisles.

On some *shinkansen* lines you need to be sure you get in the right car, since some cars are disengaged at a stop before the end of the line or are released to branch onto another route.

Limited Express Trains (Tokkyū) and Express Trains (Kyūkō)

Although not as fast as the *shinkansen*, limited express trains offer frequent service to most cities in Japan, providing wider service than the *shinkansen*. *Tokkyū* trains have the same three classes of service as the *shinkansen* and similar amenities. There is a supplemental fee charged for travel on *tokkyū* trains.

Now less common than *tokkyū* trains, many express trains, or *kyūkō*, were upgraded to limited express trains. *Kyūkō* trains are also intercity trains, and the supplement charged for them is slightly less than for *tokkyū*.

Overnight Trains (Y a k ō R e s s y a)

Overnight trains have largely been supplanted by the faster *shinkansen* and air travel. Sleeper cars are quite a bit more expensive than other train fares and many people find that the amenities do not live up to that fare. The B-class cars on older trains have couchette-type compartments with three- or two-tier berths, while newer trains are divided into smaller compartments occupied by only one or two passengers. A-class tickets are more expensive, of course, and slightly more comfortable.

Japan also has a few luxury overnight trains, although these are generally regarded more as a way to enjoy a vacation than as a means of getting from here to there. These luxury trains offer deluxe accommodations and a restaurant car.

Local Trains (F u t s ū R e s s y a)

Because the goal is to get as many people as possible from one place to another as inexpensively as possible, travel on *futsū ressya* is often not what you would call comfortable. Even in rural areas, trains can become crowded when the number of cars is kept to a minimum as a cost-saving measure.

However, local train fares are cheaper than the express or bullet train, and they stop in many of the smaller towns that the other trains bypass. They are slower than the *shinkansen, tokkyū,* and even *kyūkō*, but if you aren't in a hurry you can take the opportunity to enjoy the scenery and stop off to explore the towns along the way.

96

GETTING AROUND

Futsū ressya do not depart as frequently as the other trains, so you should be aware of the timetables.

Planes

Air travel is a quick, convenient way to get around in Japan, especially from island to island, but it is slightly more expensive than train travel. Japan has five major domestic airlines and many local operators. Japan's major airlines are Japan Air Lines (JAL), All Nippon Airways (ANA), Japan Air Systems (JAS), Air Nippon Koku (ANK), and Japan Trans Ocean Air (JTA). Each has different routes in different areas of the country, but together they cover pretty much the whole country.

If you are able to plan your travel in advance, you can get up to a 50% discount for booking a month ahead on some airlines or a smaller discount for booking one to three weeks ahead.

Buses

Although obviously slower than trains, bus travel is a viable option for intercity travel, especially with the expansion of Japan's highway infrastructure. Indeed, because the trains do not go absolutely everywhere and JR is actually closing some of its money-losing local rail routes, a bus may be the only way to get to some towns.

Buses travel along the expressways and connect with local transportation at each station stop along the way.

You can purchase bus tickets at the Green Window in major rail stations or through a travel agency.

Ferries

Most landlubbers don't think about boats for everyday travel, but Japan is, after all, a series of islands. You can take a ferry to hop down to another port on the same island or to go to one of the outlying islands. You can even take a trip from one tip of the country to the other. There are car ferries as well as passenger ferries.

Fares vary based on the distance traveled and the class of travel selected, ranging from the most basic accommodations where you toss your futon on the tatami mat floor along with the other passengers, to more luxurious—and more expensive—private cabins. Information on ferry routes, schedules, and fares can be found in the *JR Jikokuhyō* or from the local Tourist Information Center.

SAFETY

Japan is one of the safest countries to visit or live in. Despite a recent rise in reports of muggings and other crimes, these acts are still quite uncommon by U.S. standards. However, it's a bad idea to become overconfident, especially since foreigners are often the target for pickpockets and other thieves, and in Japan, most foreigners stand out like a sore thumb.

Although public transportation and most places are safe after dark, use your common sense, especially if you are traveling alone, and avoid poorly lit areas and so on.

Women should also be aware that foreign women, especially those walking alone, are sometimes subjected to fondling in crowded trains (see Tips for a Smooth Ride), propositions from drunk salarymen, and men who expose themselves.

In an Emergency

There are two telephone numbers you need to know in the event of an emergency: 110 for the police and 119 for fire or ambulance. Note, however, that these lines are not manned by bilingual operators, although you should be able to make yourself understood if necessary by sticking to basic English phrases.

An alternative for non-Japanese speakers is the Japan Hotline, which can be reached at 0120-46-1997. This helpline has English-speaking operators and is available 24 hours a day, seven days a week.

FIVE

LIVING AND STAYING IN JAPAN

Whether you're moving to Japan for several years or just staying for a few months, either on business or for personal reasons, this chapter will show you the nuts and bolts of everyday life. Here you'll learn how to avoid the pitfalls of housing, using telephones, dining, and socializing. This section contains a lot of useful information even if you're spending just a day or two in Japan, so read on. The bottom line is that you will be interacting with the Japanese on some level, no matter how long your stay. Here's how to make that interaction enjoyable for everyone.

HOUSING

If you're not planning on renting or buying a house in Japan, you may want to skip ahead to "Bringing Your Belongings."

The logistics of finding a home are complex. You have to be in Japan to rent a home, so you will need temporary lodgings while you do your hunting. You can stay in a hotel or inn, of course, but in larger cities you also have the option of serviced executive apartments, available for a couple of weeks or a couple of months while you make more permanent plans.

Many companies own apartment buildings or dormitories which they rent to their employees. These apartments are generally filled by young singles. The rent is usually much lower than it would be for a private apartment, and there is often a cafeteria or company-subsidized dining room on the premises.

In addition to these company-sponsored facilities, there are, of course, privately owned apartments and houses. Be sure that your expectations are realistic when you start your hunt for quarters. Apartments and homes in Japan tend to be expensive and very compact, with some rooms doing double duty, such as a room that serves as a living room by day and a bedroom by night.

Finding a Living Space

Once you have decided what type of place you are looking for, there are many different ways to begin your hunt. You can peruse the ads in English-language newspapers, work with a real estate broker, or try to contact the landlord or management companies of the building in which you are interested.

Because of the intricacies of locating housing as an expatriate, especially if you don't speak the language, the majority of expatriates in Japan enlist the assistance of a real estate agent (*fudōsan*). Your agent will show you available apartments for free, but expect to pay the equivalent of about one month's rent in agent's fees when you find a house or apartment. If possible, try to find an agent who has experience working with foreigners. Some real estate agents also act as property management companies; these companies are generally very willing to rent to foreigners.

If you're looking for an apartment, you will see *apāto*—apartments in smaller buildings, usually cheaper and constructed of

wood—and *manshon*—apartments in larger, concrete buildings, more modern and more expensive.

Room size is measured by how many tatami mats can be used in it. A *jō* (tatami mat) is about 1.8 m x 90 cm, so a 6-*jō* room (a common room size in Japanese homes) is about 10 square meters, or 33 square feet. An advertisement for a 1K apartment means one room (typically a 6-*jō* room) and a kitchen; 1DK means one room, dining room, and kitchen (the latter two are often combined); 1LDK means one room, living room, dining room, and kitchen.

Some landlords do refuse to rent to foreigners, so an agent who is used to handling these situations can be an invaluable asset. Keep in mind, too, that because the Japanese prefer an indirect style of communication, excessive stalling or making excuses may signal some kind of problem, such as a landlord who does not want to rent to you. It will do you no good to protest or proclaim your "rights;" landlords in Japan can, and sometimes do, refuse to rent to an applicant with no reason. Unfortunately, this often means that foreigners, seniors, people with disabilities, and students have a difficult time finding apartments.

Moving In

The cost of moving into a new home in Japan can come as quite a shock. Be prepared to shell out about six month's worth of rent before the moving truck pulls up with your belongings. You will pay one month's rent (*yachin*), the real estate agent's fee (*tesūryō*) equaling one month's rent, two months' rent as a deposit (*shikikin*), and two months' rent for "key money" (*reikin*) to the landlord (alternately referred to as an "honorarium," allegedly given to show your thanks for being allowed to rent). Note that when you leave, only the *shikikin*, or deposit, is refundable. However, your landlord can deduct from the *shikikin* based on the condition of the apartment when you move out, so don't bank on getting that money back. Most landlords require at least 30 days' notice before you move out; if you don't give sufficient notice, you may have to pay a penalty.

You will need to sign a lease for your new apartment; most leases are for two years. As a foreigner, you will be required to have a Japanese guarantor for your lease. This can be your employer or another individual. You must be physically in Japan to sign the lease, which can make it difficult to prearrange your living quarters. Many people find themselves housed in company dormitories, hotels, or guest houses while they look for a place to live.

As you would with any legal document, be sure you read the provisions of your lease thoroughly before signing it. If it is in Japanese, have it translated or, at the very least, make sure it is clearly explained to you. You may need a personal name stamp to sign the lease. These are easily obtained locally; see the section on *inkan*, or name stamps, for more details.

People moving to other countries have again and again been caught off-guard when it came time to move into their new, unfurnished homes. Generally speaking, an unfurnished apartment guarantees you nothing more than four solid walls, a floor, and a ceiling.

If your living space was inhabited when you first looked at it (if you even had the opportunity to see it in advance at all), you may have assumed that some of the items you saw there came with the apartment. Appliances that most American renters find in unfurnished apartments are not necessarily part of the deal in Japan. Many a new tenant has found himself or herself without a refrigerator or even lights upon moving in because those things belonged to the previous tenants, who naturally took them when they left. Therefore, it is important that you clarify exactly what will be in the apartment when you move in, right down to the fixtures.

Other details to discuss with your potential landlord before committing to a contract are the availability of telephone lines, utilities (gas and electricity), hot water, and heat. Air-conditioning is seldom found in Japanese homes. Your real estate agent can be an invaluable source of information and assistance when it comes time to deal with the necessities of getting set up in your new place.

UTILITIES

You will need to notify the electric, water, and gas companies when you move into your new home. You should find a card attached to or near your circuit breaker box. This card shows the last meter reading. Fill out the card with your name and other pertinent information and mail it to the electric company. You may have to switch on your electricity at the circuit breaker; if the electricity does not come on, you can call the electric company. They will send someone by to help you out and investigate any problems.

Your home may use either propane or city-provided gas. If you're on the city gas system, call the gas company to have someone come turn on the main valve. If possible, call a couple of days before you move in, since it can take two to three days to get service started. If your home uses propane, call a local propane provider to have them bring or fill your tanks.

Remember that Japan frequently experiences earthquakes. If you are at home during an earthquake, turn off electrical, gas, and propane-fueled appliances.

There should be a card in your entryway or attached to a faucet for getting the water turned on. Simply fill out the card and mail it to the waterworks bureau or call the bureau with the necessary information. You should also find instructions for turning on the main water valve if it has been shut off. Call the waterworks bureau if you can't turn on the water or if you have any questions.

You will be billed for electricity, water, sewage, and fuel. Bills for city services can be paid by direct withdrawal from your bank, at banks, post offices, and some convenience stores. Don't forget to let all utility companies know when you move so you can settle any outstanding balances and ensure that you won't be billed for the next occupant's services.

TELEPHONES

Once you've found your new home, you will need to apply for a telephone line. You are essentially buying a subscription right, which can be done at the local NTT (Nippon Telegraph & Telephone Corporation) office at a cost of about ¥75,000 plus an installation fee of around ¥2,100. This is necessary even if there is already a phone jack present. You will need to provide identification and proof of your address when you apply, so take your passport and foreign resident certificate with you. You can buy the subscription rights from a broker or the previous tenant, but you will need to provide both the seller's and the buyer's identification to the phone company and pay a transfer fee of about ¥850.

You can rent a telephone from NTT for about ¥200 to ¥300 per month, or you can buy one from a retail store.

Your phone bill will reflect a basic fee plus the cost of your phone calls. With the exception of emergency calls, every call, local or long distance, is a toll call. As with other utility bills, you can pay your monthly telephone bill by direct withdrawal from your bank account or at banks, post offices, or convenience stores.

Mobile Phones

There are two types of mobile phones in Japan: regular cell phones (*keitai denwa*) and PHS (Personal Handyphone System). Regular cell phones cover a wider calling area and reception is better in buildings, on trains, etc. However, the rates are higher than for PHS phones. Because of the wide variety of service providers and options such as e-mail and data transmission, it would be wise to investigate what each has to offer to find the one that best meets your needs. In Japan, the caller pays for the phone call in all instances.

By the Way . . .

In Japan, the public use of cellular phones (*keitai*) is frowned upon, and the implications of using them in dangerous situations is taken quite seriously. It is illegal to use *keitai* while driving. Many theaters and concert halls have "jammers" legally installed to block out *keitai* signals, preventing their use in situations where they are considered a nuisance. Be on the lookout for signs prohibiting their use on trains and in restaurants. As a general rule, if you avoid using your *keitai* in enclosed public situations, you won't offend anyone.

Public Phones and Calling Cards

You will be able to readily find a public pay phone in Japan, especially in major cities. Almost all will be in working order, since a vandalized public phone is the exception rather than the rule.

To use a pay phone, simply lift the receiver, insert your coin(s), and dial the number. A local call at a pay phone will cost ¥10 for the first three minutes; you will hear a tone when the time runs out so you can deposit more coins. Many public phones accept prepaid phone cards. Phone cards in ¥500 and ¥1,000 denominations can be purchased at convenience stores or from vending machines.

Some pay phones take different coin denominations, and some do not. Some take phone cards and some do not. Some phones are for local calls only, while others can be used to make international calls. The color of the phone indicates how it can be used. It can be a little confusing until you get used to it, but here are some general guidelines.

- Red and pink phones take only ¥10 coins.
- White, yellow, and green phones take either ¥10 or ¥100 coins.
- Green and gray phones take phone cards.

Pay phones take coins from ¥10 to ¥100. If you deposit several ¥10 coins but don't use them all, the unused ones will be returned when you complete your call, but if you insert a ¥100 coin, you may not get change if you do not use all of the allotted minutes.

For international calls, you can use a phone designated for that purpose. Look for gray ISDN phones or green phones with a gold plate on the phone pad; these are usually clearly marked as international phones. You may not find them on every street corner—your best bet is in airports or major train stations or in high-end hotels that cater to an international clientele. To use a credit card to place an international call, you will need to locate a "credit phone," which are found most often in airports or hotel lobbies.

Useful Phone Numbers

The following numbers are the same throughout Japan. Emergency operators may not speak English, so it would be helpful to learn a few basic Japanese phrases so you can get assistance if necessary. (See the Language chapter for some key emergency phrases.) If you need to make an emergency call from a public phone, press the red emergency button, then dial the appropriate emergency number.

Police: 110
Fire and ambulance: 119
Local directory assistance: 104; in English (0120) 36-4463
To request an English telephone book: (0120) 46-0815

Another number to keep handy is the Japan Hotline, which can answer inquiries in several different languages, including English, 24 hours a day. The toll free number is (0120) 46-1997.

GARBAGE REMOVAL

Unless you want to make yourself very unpopular with your neighbors, there are a few things you should know about the mundane task of taking out the garbage. There are very specific rules that you will need to learn regarding how and when to put out your garbage, but the rules do vary by community. In general, trash is separated into burnable items, such as paper and food scraps, and non-burnable materials, such as plastic. If you have a large item to get rid of, such as furniture, your community may have a scheduled day for collection or you may need to call to have the item picked up; there may be a small fee for this service.

Some communities ask that you also separate out recyclables for separate disposal. These may be collected or you may need to take them to community recycling bins. You may also be required to use a specific type of garbage can or bag. If your garbage is not correctly separated, it may be left at the curb by the garbage collectors. If you will be living in an apartment building, ask the landlord or your neighbors how you should dispose of garbage and recyclables. If you will be living in a house or if you need more information, contact your community's sanitation department for general information and instructions for disposing of particular items.

REGISTERING

Foreigners who stay more than 90 days will need to register with the Japanese government to obtain a *Gaikokujin Tōrokushō* (Alien Registration Card). You can apply at the local government office for your district or town. Be sure to take your passport as identification; you will also need to supply two passport-sized photos with your application. You'll receive a temporary certificate immediately and will be notified when your permanent card is ready, usually after four weeks or so. Once you are in possession of your registration card, you should carry it with you at all times; this rule applies to all foreigners 16 years old and older. You may need to produce the card for the police, and if you don't have it with you, you may be fined or even detained. If you move to a new address, have a change in your visa status, or renew your visa, you must notify the local government of the change within 14 days. If you lose your registration card, you will need to reapply for it within 14 days of loss. When you are leaving the country at the end of your stay, you will surrender your registration card to an immigration officer at the airport.

GETTING AN INKAN (NAME SEAL)

Name seals or stamps are used in place of a handwritten signature in most cases in Japan. Until you are able to get an *inkan*, you can ask if you can use your written signature instead; this will suffice for many of your initial transactions, such as opening a bank account. *Inkan* are used for every legal transaction, opening accounts, and signing everyday documents, so it's a good idea to put getting an *inkan* high on your to-do list when you arrive.

There are several different types of seals, so you may end up with two or more stamps that will be used for different purposes. A *mitome-in* is a stamp that is used for general purposes, such as receiving packages. A *ginkō-in* is a bank seal that is used to open bank accounts, set up direct deposits, and perform other financial transactions. *Jitsu-in* are seals that are registered with the government, used for legally binding contracts, such a real estate or automobile purchases. Because *jitsu-in* are registered with the government, it's a good idea to check with your local municipal office for any rules or restrictions before having one carved.

While the same stamp can be used for all three, there can be serious consequences if a *ginkō-in* or *jitsu-in* is lost or stolen and misused, so most people have at least two *inkan*, one for everyday use and one for more weighty matters. It's important to remember that an *inkan* is the equivalent of a legal signature, so don't treat it lightly. Make sure that you keep it in a safe place, especially *ginkō-in* and *jitsu-in* seals.

BRINGING YOUR BELONGINGS

There are many things to take into consideration when you are deciding what to take with you to Japan and what to leave behind. Keep in mind that many of your electronics and appliances will not work in Japan without modification. Perhaps the most important consideration, however, is the fact that Japanese housing tends to be very small when compared to the U.S., so that huge antique sideboard is probably not going to fit into your new dining room.

Appliances and Computers

Electricity in Japan is 100 volts everywhere. However, the eastern half of the country, which includes Tokyo, is on a 50 Hertz system and the

western half, including Osaka, Kyoto, and Nagoya, uses 60 Hertz. This is compared to the 110 volts, 60 Hertz that is standard in the U.S. Most American appliances will work without a current converter, but if you live in a 50 Hertz area, the timing may be off in some appliances, such as clocks, vacuum cleaners, microwaves or CD players. Do check your appliances before you plug them in; ask at an electronics or appliance store if you are unsure. Plugging them into an outlet with the wrong voltage and frequency can damage your appliances and electronic equipment.

The shape of your plug may also be an obstacle. On U.S. plugs, one blade is generally longer than the other; this is a safety feature designed to reduce the possibility of an accidental shock. Many outlets in Japan are designed for plugs with blades of equal thickness and cannot accept the larger blade. In addition, some outlets do not have a third hole for the grounding pin. Although these problems are easily solved by using plug adapters, you may end up needing multiple adapters. In the best-case scenario, you will have found your new house or apartment before you move your belongings, and will be better able to gauge which appliances you can take with you and what modifications, if any, are necessary.

If you decide not to take your own appliances, there are several options for finding appliances locally. For example, you can look into buying them from other people who are leaving the country. There are also companies that specialize in providing appliances that meet local requirements to people moving overseas. Some of these companies are listed in Appendix B.

PETS

Before deciding to bring your pet with you when you move to Japan, it's important to know that pets are not allowed in most apartments. Even if you have found pet-friendly housing, bringing a pet into Japan will take some planning. Like you, your pet will have to have the proper papers for entry into the country. You will need to get a

health certificate and a rabies inoculation certificate for your pet; both documents must be endorsed within 30 days of issuance by the U.S. Department of Agriculture (or equivalent administrative department if you're moving from another country), but within 10 days of your arrival in Japan.

Your pet will need to have a rabies shot at least 30 days before entering Japan; if your pet has already had a rabies shot, make sure it won't expire before you leave for Japan. Even with a rabies shot, your cat or dog will need to be quarantined, at your expense, for at least two weeks at a cost of around ¥2,500 per day. If your pet's rabies shot has expired or if the shot was received within the 30-day window, the quarantine will be longer, up to 180 days in the former case.

For more information on bringing your pet into Japan, check with the Japanese Consulate in your country.

BRINGING OR BUYING A VEHICLE

Even if you are attached to old Betsy, it is not recommended that you bring your vehicle to Japan. The most obvious problem is that, unless you are moving from the United Kingdom, Australia, or New Zealand, your car is not properly configured: Japanese cars have the steering wheel on the right side of the car.

Beyond that, however, there are a host of other obstacles. Vehicles more than three years old have to pass an inspection (*shaken*) every two years that is both stringent and expensive, costing about ¥10,000. Once the vehicle hits nine years, it has to be inspected every year. Add to that the expense of renting a mandatory off-street parking space, an annual tax of up to ¥56,000 based on the size of your car, insurance, and the high cost of gasoline and the bright prospect of owning a car is likely to dull significantly. On top of all this, consider traffic that moves slower than a snail's pace in Tokyo and other big cities, and you will probably abandon not only any plans to bring your own car to Japan, but the entire idea of owning a car at all. Most people living in Japan's cities find that the public transportation system is quite sufficient for their daily needs, and less of a hassle than owning a car. After all, you can always rent a car for those exploratory trips or weekend getaways.

If these costs and challenges don't deter you from wanting to buy a car during your stay in Japan, you may want to consider a used car or a *kei* (microcar). If you are going to be staying only a short while, you may be able to find a bargain on a used car, especially if it is unlikely to pass its next *shaken*. So, for example, if you are on a 12-month assignment, you can buy a used car that is due for inspection in 16 months. Note, however, that when you are ready to ditch the car at the end of your stay, you may have to pay to have someone pick up the car to be scrapped.

If you just need a little car to tool around in, a microcar, which has a 660 cc or smaller engine and is less than 330 cm (10 ft 10 in) long and 140cm (4 ft 7 in) wide, may interest you. Microcars are exempt from having to rent off-street parking and, since the annual tax is based on the size of the vehicle and your gas mileage will be good, your annual expenses will be less.

When you buy a car in Japan, you will have to pay a 5% consumption tax and an additional acquisition tax ranging from around ¥56,000 to ¥75,600. You will need to have at least basic mandatory insurance for your car and can add on optional insurance to cover personal injury, theft, disaster, and so forth.

To learn the basic rules of the road for driving in Japan, whether in your own car or a rental, please refer to the Getting Around chapter in this book. For specific details and costs for bringing your vehicle into Japan, check with the Japanese Consulate in your country.

SCHOOLS

If you have children, one of your priorities will be to find a school that will meet their academic needs. There are three options in Japan: local schools, American schools offering an American curriculum, and international schools. There are many things to take into consideration, including your child's age, language proficiency, and what kind of curriculum is best for your child. The choice of a school is a very individual one, so you will need to weigh the pros and cons of each of your options.

Children of foreign residents are eligible to attend local Japanese public schools. Instruction, of course, is in Japanese; Japanese students begin learning English when they reach the junior high school level. In addition, the Japanese teaching and learning methods will be as foreign to non-Japanese students as the language. Local schools may be a good way to immerse younger children in the experience of living in Japan, but older children are likely to have considerable difficulties unless they already speak Japanese. You will also need to think ahead to how your child's learning in Japan, in terms of the curriculum, language skills, and teaching methods, will affect his or her reentry into the school system in your home country when your assignment is over. You can find more information on the Japanese school system in the Background chapter.

International and foreign-community (American, Canadian, etc.) schools have curricula specifically designed to provide continuity for children, both for when they come to Japan as well as for when they leave and must reintegrate into their home school systems. Students in these schools come from many different countries, so your child will have even more exposure to other cultures. In Japan's larger cities, you will have many schools to choose from. The list of schools serving the expatriate community in Tokyo, for example, includes Montessori, Catholic, Christian, American, Canadian, and international schools. International and foreign-community schools are private, so tuition fees will apply; scholarships are available from some schools.

You can do much of your research on schools in your new city before you go by checking the Internet for various schools' Web sites and expatriate community Web sites.

SHOPPING

You will have a wide variety of shops and goods to choose from, ranging from huge department stores to small specialty shops. However, it is expensive to live in Japan and this extends to groceries and other everyday purchases. Credit cards are accepted in a growing list of department stores, but cash is still the payment of choice.

Shops in Japan tend to close at around 7:00 PM. If you need something after hours, however, you shouldn't have any trouble finding one of the 24-hour convenience stores that are popping up everywhere. Of course, that convenience will cost you a bit more.

As you walk around, you will notice the proliferation of vending machines. These sell mainly drinks, including beer and alcohol, magazines, and snacks.

Unless you are going to a very remote area, you will be able to find most of the foods you are accustomed to, including major U.S. brands. You may find, though, that even though a product carries a familiar brand it may be slightly different, since formulas are often modified to suit Japanese tastes. For example, many products are not

as sweet as they are in the United States, so a cola or cereal my not be exactly what your taste buds are expecting.

Supermarkets are becoming quite common in Japan and carry a wide variety of food and other daily necessities. You will also have the option of buying fresh food and produce at a specialty store, such as the fishmonger's or greengrocer's.

Department stores offer the largest selection of goods, from inexpensive items to top-of-the-line goods. Many department stores also have a food store in the basement. Department stores are popular destinations for people shopping for one of the ubiquitous gifts that are given throughout the year. Be forewarned that during *ochūgen* and *oseibo*, the major gift-giving times in July and December, hordes of people flock to department stores in search of the perfect gift. When you need to add an *ochūgen*, *oseibo*, or other gift to the shopping list, you can refer to the section on Gifts in this chapter for pointers.

Buying clothing in Japan can be difficult. Since clothing is made to fit the typical Japanese physique, most Westerners, especially those who wear large sizes or are tall, find that the clothing doesn't fit particularly well. Big- and tall-sized clothing is not found on every street corner and, when you do find it, it is usually quite expensive. Ordering from a catalog or Web site can be a good solution, but be sure you factor in the costs of shipping and customs for the items.

For the most part, bargaining is not appropriate in Japan. The one exception is in the electronics district in major cities, such as Tokyo's Akihabara district. Even so, don't expect loud voices or waving of the arms. Instead, the way to get a few yen shaved off the price is to make a polite request, which will often result in about a 10% reduction in the price.

FINANCIAL MATTERS

Japan's currency is the yen (¥). Paper notes come in denominations of ¥10,000, ¥5,000, and ¥1,000. Notes with a new look were issued in 1984, but you may still see the older notes; both versions are legal tender. Coin denominations are 500, 100, 50, 10, 5, and 1 yen. ¥100 and ¥10 coins are the useful for vending machines and pay phones.

Although credit card use is steadily increasing in major cities, especially in larger department stores, hotels, and high-end restau-

rants, most smaller establishments and supermarkets accept cash only. Checks are virtually unheard of. This means you may have to carry around a lot more cash that you are used to. The good news is that it's generally safe to do so in Japan.

It can be difficult to find an ATM that will accept a foreign debit card, especially outside of major cities; you will have the best luck if your ATM is part of the PLUS or Cirrus system. Note that not all ATMs are open 24 hours a day; some are only open until 6:00 or 9:00 PM.

If you're using travelers' checks or need to change cash, you can go to an "Authorized Foreign Exchange Bank" or a major post office. Major international hotels can often exchange currency or cash traveler's checks as well.

Monthly bills can be paid in person at the post office, at convenience stores or directly through your bank by automatic withdrawal. For automatic withdrawal, simply fill out the necessary form from the utility company, the phone company, or other service provider authorizing monthly payments. Each month the appropriate amount will be transferred from your account to the payee and you will receive a receipt of the amount withdrawn. You can still dispute charges if you have a problem, and you can discontinue this service at any time. Just be sure you have enough money in the account; you'll be charged a fee if the bill is paid and the funds are not available.

As mentioned in the section on name seals, in most banks you can open a bank account without a seal, since you are a foreigner, but some do require an *inkan* or name seal.

As an alternative to a bank, you can open an account at the post office. The basic services, such as bill payment and ATM use, are similar to a bank account.

PERSONAL HYGIENE

You will find when you are in Japan that the facilities for taking care of your most basic needs, the toilet and bath, are quite different from what you are used to in the U.S. In most cases, the toilet is separated from the bathing area.

In some hotels, public toilets, and homes you may find Western-style or both Japanese and Western toilets. A Japanese-style toilet is an elongated oval with a hood over one end. One does not sit on this type of toilet; one squats over it, facing the hooded end. This can be a little tricky to master if you are not used to it. Remind yourself to check to make sure nothing will fall out of your pockets before using a Japanese toilet.

If there are slippers just inside the door to the toilet, a common practice in homes and small inns where the bathroom is shared, they are for use in the toilet only. Remove the slippers you are wearing in the house, setting them outside the bathroom door, and put on the slippers before taking care of business; remember to change back before you leave.

The door to the toilet may not have a lock in some homes. Look for slippers outside the door, signaling that the toilet is occupied. Knock before entering as well. If you're in the bathroom, public or private, when someone knocks, knock back to indicate that it is occupied.

There may not be towels or toilet paper in public toilets. Most people carry a handkerchief for when they need the former and/or tissue paper for the latter.

A typical bathing area will contain a deep, square tub, as well as a tiled area equipped with a faucet and shower head, stool and bowl. The water in the tub is very hot and is used for soaking, not for lathering up with soap or shampoo. You will do your washing sitting on a small stool in the tiled area near the faucet or shower and then rinse thoroughly before stepping into the tub. Because the washing is done outside the tub, everyone in the family can enjoy a nice, relaxing soak without having to drain and refill the tub.

Public baths (*sentō*) do still exist in Japan and you may have occasion to visit one. You will usually be given a small bowl to hold your soap and washcloth and will place your clothes in a locker. The rules for public baths are similar to the ones mentioned above: the hot water is for soaking, not washing, so sit on one of the small stools in the designated area to wash up and rinse yourself thoroughly before getting into the tub.

ETIQUETTE

It's important to familiarize yourself with Japanese etiquette before you hit the ground. Japan is a country with numerous rituals, big and small, that prescribe the proper interaction between two people in almost every circumstance. But don't let this intimidate you unduly. One of the benefits of being a foreigner is that you are allowed a great deal of latitude for the occasional faux pas. In fact, you will find that most Japanese will go out of their way to make you feel comfortable. Simply acting courteously toward others will go a long way. It can be extremely helpful to find a Japanese friend or an experienced expatriate who can guide you through the waters.

Japanese Names

In Japan, names are written with the surname first, followed by the given name. The Japanese are not as quick to use first names as their Western counterparts, especially Americans. Even people who have known one another for years will refer to each other by their last names. Children and family members may use first names or nicknames; adults who have known each other since childhood may do so as well.

It is most polite in all circumstances to use the person's last name, followed by the honorific -*san*; this applies to both men and women (i.e., Kazawa-*san*). Teachers, professors, and instructors are called *sensei*. *Sensei* can be used alone or added to the person's last name (i.e., Itō *sensei*). In an office environment, a person's title is often used in lieu of the name when speaking of someone or addressing him or her directly. Examples are *shachō* (president) and *buchō* (department head). Do not add -*san* to these titles.

You should never take the liberty of calling someone by their first name unless invited. You may find that Japanese contacts and colleagues who have extensive experience with the U.S. are comfortable with the use of first names, and may ask you to call them by their first name. However, it's important to remember that this courtesy should apply to informal situations only. When you are in a meeting or when you are referring to that person in conversation, you should use the person's last name.

Meeting and Greeting

Bowing is a very important part of Japanese life. Bows are used to greet someone, to take your leave, to say thank you, to apologize, and at numerous other times during your daily routine. Interestingly enough, bowing is such an ingrained habit that you will even see people bowing when they talk to someone on the phone.

Most Japanese have grown accustomed to shaking hands with Westerners and will initiate a handshake; some people will both bow or nod and shake hands with you. When they do shake hands, you will find that the Japanese handshake is usually soft; be sure you don't pump or squeeze too enthusiastically. A Japanese person with extensive experience dealing with foreigners may make eye contact with you as he shakes your hand, but since that is bad manners in Japan, it is more likely that he will not. Japanese women do not usually shake hands.

There is more to bowing than just bending at the waist. The formality of the bow—the depth of the bend and placement of the hands—is dependent on the relationship between the two people. For most bows, you should stand with your feet together and your hands at your sides; bow from the waist. An informal bow should take you down about 15°, a semiformal bow about 30°. For the most formal bow, place your hands on the front of your legs and let them slide down as you bend to about 45°. Very often people are standing close together when they bow, and dipping straight down is likely to garner you a bump on the head, so bow slightly to the right.

Don't worry; it's not necessary to get out your protractor. What is important that you show respect for people and for their position, not that your bow is exactly 30° or 45°.

These bows, of course, assume that you are in a standing position and are appropriate for most greetings. However, when you enter someone's home, much of the greetings will require bowing from a kneeling position. Please refer to the section in this chapter entitled "Be My Guest: Being on Your Best Behavior as a Host or Guest."

When two people who don't know each other meet for the first time, they usually make a shallow bow as they exchange business cards. As they read each other's card, they get an idea of their status vis-à-vis one another and then they bow again with the correct level of formality.

Chance meetings, such as seeing a friend on the sidewalk or passing a co-worker in the hall, do not require great formality. A friend or work peer whom you see often can be greeted with a wave as you pass; superiors only slightly above you can be greeted in passing with a brief nod. For those who are much higher above you on the totem pole, it's proper to stop before making a slight bow.

Salespeople and wait staff may bow to you in thanks for your patronage, but you need only nod back.

Communicating

You may find that you are asked some rather personal questions, including what your salary is, if you are married and, if not, why. Don't be offended; most likely the person is simply trying to show interest. If you feel a question is too personal, give a vague answer. For example, if you are asked how much you make, you can reply that it's not as much as your kids spend.

As described in the Culture chapter, the Japanese are indirect communicators. Don't expect them to come out and say "no." When you hear phrases such as "maybe," they can usually be interpreted as a negative.

It's considered immature to lose your temper, so try to keep a cool head when you get angry or frustrated. It's also poor manners to brag, so keep your tone and your words modest.

Remember that jokes do not travel well. Puns and double entendres don't translate and references to events or icons of your home country are often not understood. Especially avoid sexual or political jokes. Also avoid the American propensity to start a presentation with a joke to break the ice.

Out and About

Following is a roundup of a few other miscellaneous points that will show that you have good manners. Don't chew gum, especially in a business setting; this is considered extremely rude. Keep your hands out of your pockets while you are talking to someone.

Public displays of affection, including hand holding, are rarely seen in Japan. While you will see young people holding hands and even making out in public, most people prefer a bit more decorum.

Although you will see many street vendors, you shouldn't eat while walking down the street. If you buy something from a vendor, you can eat it standing nearby or save it to eat later.

You will notice that the extremely polite Japanese can seem extremely impolite when push comes to shove: during rush hour. Trains are crammed way past capacity, traffic is horrendous, and the streets are crowded. People will jostle, push, and shove to squeeze in before the doors close.

The Japanese are not unfriendly, but they don't generally smile at or greet strangers on the street, in stores (except for sales staff, of course), on the train, in elevators, etc.

GIFTS

Gift-giving is an important custom in Japan, both socially and in a business environment. There are many occasions for giving gifts, dictated either by the calendar, events in one's life, or specific circumstances. No matter what the reason for the gift, it creates an obligation for the recipient, usually to return a gift or favor of some type. As a foreigner, you are given plenty of leeway to make mistakes, so don't feel like you have to be spot-on for every occasion. It really is the thought that counts in almost every case, and the fact that you take the time to learn about Japanese customs is a gift in and of itself, even if you bungle a time or two.

Certain occasions, such as weddings and funerals, call for gifts of money, while others require a trip to the department store to select a special gift. Some specific suggestions follow, but do remember that all gifts should be appropriate to the occasion, correctly wrapped, and guidelines regarding colors and numbers taken into account. If you are unsure how much money to place in a wedding envelope or what to send when your boss's wife has a baby, ask for guidance from a friend, colleague, or even the salesperson at a department store.

Although it's nice to present your gifts in person, it's often impractical, so it's perfectly fine to have the gift delivered to the recipient's home. Most stores will wrap and deliver the gift for you; you need only pick it out, pay, and provide the address.

Ochūgen and Oseibo

Japan has two major gift-giving times: *ochūgen* at the end of June through early July and *oseibo* at the end of November through the middle of December. It's probably no accident that these coincide with the twice-annual bonuses that you will receive. Unfortunately for many people, the cost of their gift-giving obligations eats up a large chunk of those bonuses.

During *ochūgen* and *oseibo*, people give gifts as a way of showing appreciation for assistance or patronage. Businesses send gifts to their clients, workers give gifts to their bosses, students give gifts to their teachers, and individuals give gifts to relatives or other people who have helped them along the way. For example, someone in a middle management position may give a gift to a superior who has acted as a mentor, to a professor from his university days, to a colleague at work who has been particularly supportive, and to an uncle who helped him financially through some hard times. And that may be just the beginning of a very long list. On the other hand, if you're the boss, you may find yourself the recipient of a pile of gifts, quantities of teas, saké, and other things in daunting abundance.

There are many suitable gifts for *ochūgen* and *oseibo*, including tea, coffee, wine, brandy, whiskey, saké, seaweed, candy, cookies, meats, jams, cheese, fish, fruit, soy sauce, and bath soaps. These times generate peak sales at stores, so you will find specially packaged gifts almost everywhere. Keep in mind, though, that where you buy the gift will make as much of an impression as what you buy.

It can be tricky to know how much to spend on a gift because there are so many variables. You will need to consider the nature of your relationship and, of course, what you can afford. Generally speaking, *ochūgen* and *oseibo* gifts range from about ¥3,000 to ¥5,000. It's not necessary to go overboard; the act of giving is what is important and being overgenerous can result in the recipient feeling an imbalance in the relationship.

Other Gift-Giving Occasions

There are many milestones in life that invite gift giving. Luckily, custom also dictates the type of gift to give and the value of the gift. For most occasions, you can go to any department store and find an appropriate gift, nicely packaged for just that purpose.

There are births, starting a new level of school, graduations, weddings, and funerals. In addition, a little girl's third and seventh years and boys' third and fifth years are generally gift-giving occasions—not on the child's birthday, but at the Shichi-Go-San Festival in November. Appropriate gifts for these occasions are listed in the following chart.

Occasion	Gift
Birth of a baby	Clothes or toys
Starting elementary school or university	Books or other school-related items
Graduation	Cash
Weddings	Cash
Funeral	Cash (called *kōden*, or "incense money") can be taken to the wake or funeral, or sent to the family
7th, 5th, and 3rd birthday (*shichi-go-san*)	Cash (given by family members and close friends only)

Birthdays are not customarily celebrated with a party; everyone's birthday was celebrated with the new year. However, birthday parties have become prevalent for children.

If you go on a trip, whether within Japan or abroad, for business or pleasure, it's a nice gesture to bring back small gifts for your co-workers. These can be small souvenirs, and price ranges are not proscribed, so the giving is not a formal affair.

Gift Dos and Don'ts

Luckily, you can have your gifts wrapped at the store where you buy them or get assistance in selecting an appropriate envelope for a cash gift. Do ask for assistance, rather than grabbing the paper or envelope you think is prettiest, since everything from the elaborateness to the color carries added significance.

Gifts are first wrapped in regular wrapping paper, then covered with white paper. Pastel colors are popular for the inner wrapping. Be sure to avoid black for most gifts, as it is a color associated with funerals. The gifts are then tied with a *mizuhiki* made of paper strings. These strings are red and white for happy occasions, gold and silver or gold and red for weddings, and black and white for funerals. On informal gifts, you may see graphics of the *mizuhiki* printed on white paper in lieu of the actual strings.

If your gift is money, be sure to give cash, not a check. The money should be put in a special gift envelope, called a *noshibukuro*, for presentation. You can find these envelopes at stationery or department stores, or even in convenience stores. The appearance of the envelope should reflect its contents; don't buy the most elaborate envelope you see for a token cash gift or put a very generous gift in a nondescript envelope.

Gift envelopes come with pre-tied *mizuhiki* in colors similar to those mentioned above according to the occasion. There will be an appropriate inscription, such as "congratulations" or "in prayer" above the *mizuhiki* and, on gifts for formal occasions, a folded paper decoration called a *noshi* or a graphic of this.

Be sure, too, that the envelope is appropriate to the occasion.

For example, there are special envelopes that should be used only for funerals; these envelopes are black and white or black and silver, and the mizuhiki knots are opposite those used for happy occasions. It would be terribly insensitive to bring a festive envelope to a funeral or, conversely, a solemn envelope to a celebration such as a wedding.

Take care that you take into consideration superstitions regarding numbers when you select gifts. The numbers four and nine are generally regarded as inauspicious because they sound like the words for death and hardship, respectively. This means that you shouldn't give a golfer a four-pack of golf balls or have nine flowers in the bouquet you bring to your hosts. On the other hand, one, three, five, and seven are good numbers, so you can just add one extra golf ball to make your gift perfectly acceptable.

For business, avoid giving cheap gifts. If you give a gift featuring your company's logo, make sure it is small and discreet, not splashed across the item in huge neon letters.

Giving and Receiving

In Japan, gifts are given and received with both hands, accompanied by a bow. If you are the giver, be modest, perhaps mentioning that it is a "small token." The receiver often refuses to accept the gift two or three times before accepting, so be prepared to gently insist. Gifts are generally not opened in front of the giver, and wrapping is not shredded in the haste to get to the goodies. Treat the wrapping as part of the gift and undo the package carefully.

A thank-you note is called for when you receive a gift and, in most cases, you should give a return gift that is valued at about half of the original gift. The latter practice can be tricky, because the "gift" may be in the form of a favor or an actual gift. You don't need to keep a stack of pre-wrapped gifts behind your door, ready to be shoved into the hands of whoever gives you a gift. The return gift need not be given immediately, but do keep a mental list of what you have received so that you can reciprocate at a later date. For example, if you are given a gift at *ochūgen*, you may want to give that person a gift at *oseibo*.

SOCIALIZING

Meeting People and Making Friends

It can be difficult meeting people and making friends in any new location, and it's no different in Japan. The fact that many Japanese work long hours and spend what little free time they have with their families means that it will take extra effort to make friends. But it is far from impossible.

The Japanese generally work long hours and many spend hours a day commuting great distances to their jobs. As a result, they don't have a great deal of leisure time. Coworkers often share a drink and complain about bosses after work. Popular venues are bars, especially karaoke bars. If you are invited to go to a karaoke bar, leave your inhibitions at the door. You don't have to sing well or even be able to carry a tune, really; you'll win people over just by getting up and giving it a shot, even if you feel like you're making a spectacle of yourself.

If you work for a large company, you may find that it has organized clubs or sports teams that employees and sometimes family members can participate in. Many communities also have sports and cultural centers where you can take classes, or take part in an activity that interests you.

Expatriates will find expatriate clubs in many cities. These clubs offer opportunities to socialize with your fellow sojourners and may be a good way to find mentors and cultural guides, not to mention being a ready-made business network.

One good general rule of thumb for meeting people anywhere is to simply do what you like to do. A photography buff with a camera around his neck may find himself striking up a conversation with other picture takers, a painter may find that his easel draws some attention.

Be My Guest: Being on Your Best Behavior as a Host or Guest

Although a great deal of entertaining in Japan is done in restaurants, there may come a time when you receive an invitation to visit a Japanese home. There are a few things to know that will make both you and your host feel more comfortable. You may find that when you arrive, things are more relaxed than you expected, especially with contemporaries or after you have known someone for some time. Nevertheless, it's best to be aware of what is likely to occur in more formal situations. After all, it's better to err on the side of formality—your Japanese hosts can encourage you to be more informal, but they will hardly let you know if you need to put a bit more starch in your shirt.

If you have been invited to the home, it's good manners to remove your coat before you ring or knock. When the door is answered, you should bow. You may already know that shoes are not worn inside the typical Japanese home. There will be a small area just inside the door where you leave your shoes before stepping up into the house. Slip out of one shoe and step up while slipping out of the other. Since the idea is not to track dirt into the house, don't set your foot down on the lower level when you remove your shoes. Once your shoes are off, turn them around so they will be ready for you to slip back on when you leave. Make sure to leave them neatly placed side by side. Your hosts will provide a pair of slippers for you to wear inside the house.

By the Way . . .

SLIP ON, SLIP OFF

It's more practical to wear loafers or another type of slip-on shoe when you visit a Japanese home. They will be infinitely easier to remove and put back on than lace-up shoes.

Seating arrangements are very important. Where the seat of honor is will depend on the setup of the room. If there is a *tokonoma* (alcove for displaying art), the seat of honor is in front of it. If there is no *tokonoma*, the seat of honor is usually the one furthest from the door or with the best view of the garden.

Wait to be invited to take a seat. If you are not pointed to a specific seat, don't assume that you should take the seat of honor. Select a less important seat; your host may then usher you into the seat of honor. You may find yourself directed to a cushion or *zaisu* (chair with a back but no legs). The proper way to sit on these is to kneel. The formal position is to fold your legs under you, with your feet together under your rear end. Your hosts will probably quickly invite you to relax, which means that men can sit cross legged and women can tuck their legs to the side instead of underneath.

If your hosts bring someone into the room to introduce to you, such as a spouse, the proper thing to do is to move from your seat to kneel directly on the *tatami* floor and lean forward at the waist in a bow until your hands lightly touch the floor in front of you. Think of it as the Japanese version of standing up when someone enters the room. If you are being formally introduced to someone, it's proper to place your hands on the floor in front of you and bow from the waist until your forehead touches your hands.

Don't expect to be invited to see the whole house, and don't take the initiative and go off exploring. Some Japanese homes have a *tokonoma*, a small alcove where artwork, scrolls, flower arrangements, or other pieces are displayed. Feel free to approach the item or ask your hosts about it, but be careful not to step into the alcove itself. Don't overdo your admiration for any one object, or you may find yourself in an awkward position with your host trying to give it to you as a gift. Some homes have Buddhist or Shinto shrines as well.

As a guest, it's your duty to allow your host to provide hospitality; you aren't expected, for example, to help with the preparations for dinner or washing dishes afterward. Because hospitality doesn't include rushing someone out of your home, it's unlikely that your hosts will give you overt signals that it's time for you to leave. If there are other guests, you can follow their lead. Otherwise, you will have to use your own best judgment so you don't overstay your welcome.

A thank-you note is always an appropriate follow-up to a dinner or stay at someone's home.

Dating and Beyond

Intercultural relationships can be very exciting and rewarding, but they can also be complex and can require a great deal of effort. Singles entering the dating scene in Japan will have to contend with stereotypes, both their own and on the part of the Japanese. A Western man may have visions of a compliant, subservient, very feminine woman, a sort of geisha complex, if you will. For her part, a Japanese woman may expect that a Western man will be more open about expressing emotion and have a more liberal attitude toward women than Japanese men. Western women are often pleasantly surprised to discover that not all Japanese men are as distant, uncommunicative, and chauvinistic as they are often painted to be, while Japanese men soon discover that not all Western women are overbearing and overly aggressive.

One of the most difficult aspects of dating in Japan is that many people simply do not have a lot of time to socialize; it's not uncommon for people to meet their partners at work, since that's where many people spend the most of their time. For example, a Japanese salaryman may work until 10:00 in the evening on Monday through Friday or go out drinking with coworkers and spend many Saturdays working or playing golf with superiors or clients. This leaves precious little time to nurture a budding relationship.

Dating for Japanese teenagers and young adults begins somewhat later than in most Western countries. Adolescents and young teens tend to socialize in groups; it's unusual to see them dating as a couple or going steady. Gender roles remain traditional when one does begin dating, with the man footing the bill for dinner, a movie, or other activities. In public, couples tend to limit displays of affection. Although you will see the occasional young couple locked in a passionate embrace, there is little hugging, kissing, or even hand-holding in public. Even when one marries, there is typically little direct communication of affection. If you are of a more overtly passionate nature, you may have to curb your natural instincts. For example, even "*Suki desu*" ("I like you") is a strong statement.

If you do end up finding Mr. or Ms. Right while you are in Japan and want to get married there, you will need to register your marriage at the local municipal office. The Japanese spouse must provide an official copy of his or her *koseki-tōhon* (family register). The foreign spouse will need to have ready his or her passport, alien registration certificate, *gaikokujin tōroku-zumishōmei-sho* (a certificate verifying registration as an alien in the ward of residence), and *kon-in gubi shōmeisho* (an official document from his or her embassy or consulate confirming legal competency to marry).

Weddings

The custom of arranged marriages does still exist in Japan, but the majority of young people make that decision for themselves. If a marriage is being arranged, a *miai kekkon* (go-between) may introduce the two people. Even in non-arranged marriages, a *miai kekkon* is called on at some point to act as a liaison and often as a mediator between the two families in making the decisions about the wedding and reception. It's not uncommon for the groom's boss to act as the *miai kekkon*.

The first step on the path to marriage is the *yuinō* (formal engagement ceremony), when betrothal gifts are exchanged by the two families. The wedding itself is a short ceremony attended only by relatives and a few close friends, followed by a large reception with a sit-down dinner. Most guests are invited to the reception only, so don't feel like the bride and groom are making a bid for extra gifts if you aren't invited to the wedding ceremony.

If you're invited to a wedding reception, it's customary to give a gift of cash—use new bills—in a special envelope called a *shūgi-bukuro*. Place the bills in the inner envelope and write your name and the amount of your gift on this envelope before slipping it in the outer envelope. You can get envelopes made specifically for this purpose at stationery or department stores. The amount you give to the newlyweds depends on your age, financial status, and relationship to the happy couple. As an example, a younger business person might give a colleague or client ¥20,000, whereas an older, higher-ranking person might give ¥30,000. If you do go to the reception, take only your cash gift; it isn't necessary to bring an additional gift for the couple's home.

If you are not able to attend the reception, you can send a telegram and a cash gift to the couple before or within a few months of the ceremony. To send the telegram, call 115 to have it billed to your home phone or go to the post office to fill out a form. You can find appropriate congratulatory phrases in your phone book to make things easier. Your cash gift can be smaller if you aren't attending.

Customary apparel for men attending a wedding reception is a formal black suit with a white shirt and white or silver tie. Women will wear a formal *kimono*, often black with a gold or red design. If you don't have anything that formal, don't feel like you have to run out and buy a *kimono* or dinner jacket. It's okay for men to wear a black or other dark colored suit and women to wear a nice dress or suit. Men should not wear black ties, since that is what is worn to funerals, and women should not wear a white dress, which is the bride's color.

Wedding receptions are planned down to the last detail, so be sure you arrive a few minutes before the stated time. There will be a reception table outside the door where guests sign the guest book and leave their gift envelopes. You will receive a program that gives the seating arrangements and the agenda for the reception.

Shortly after everyone is seated, the go-between will formally introduce and toast the newly married couple; drinking, eating, singing, toasting, and speeches follow. You won't be called on spontaneously to make a speech, but if you were approached before the wedding and invited to say a few words, keep your speech short and polite. Unlike in the U.S., the toasters do not make fun of the newlyweds.

Expect to stay a good two to three hours at the reception. Near your chair you'll find a package, which is your *hikidemono* (return gift), containing small gifts from the bride and groom.

The above paragraphs describe a formal wedding reception, but many young people today choose to celebrate with a more casual reception that is more akin to a large party than a formal affair.

Funerals

When there is a death, there is usually a viewing, wake, and funeral, followed by cremation and internment. There will be other memorial ceremonies throughout the following year as well that are attended by the family only. As an acquaintance, you can attend either the wake or the funeral, which are held on consecutive days.

Do not go to the viewing unless you are specifically invited to do so. If you are invited to a viewing and don't wish to go, be sensitive in declining, perhaps saying that you are too sad to do so. If you do attend a viewing, first sit formally on the *tatami* and bow to the family of the deceased. There will be a white cloth covering the face of the deceased. Wait for one of the family members to lift the cloth, then lean forward to look at the face of the deceased, then bow deeply. Finally, slide back and bow again to the family before taking your leave.

Mourners bring a condolence gift of cash (*kōden*), placed in a special envelope (*kōden-bukuro*), to the wake or funeral. As always, the amount of the gift depends on your relationship to the deceased and your own circumstances. You can ask a friend or colleague for guidance in determining how much to give. If you are planning on attending both the wake and the funeral, you do not need to bring two condolence gifts.

The wake is held the evening before the funeral, usually at the home of the deceased. It's a service, so be sure you arrive on time; the same holds true for the funeral. In both cases, there will be a reception table near the entrance where you can sign the guest book and present your condolence gift. If there is no reception area, you can approach the head mourner to offer your condolences and ask where you can leave your gift.

The rituals of the wake and funeral depend on the religion of the deceased. Mourners make individual offerings of incense (Buddhist), carnations or chrysanthemums (Christian), or twigs (Shinto).

The rituals are quite simple; just pay attention to the other guests and follow their lead.

A light dinner may be served after the wake. Unless you are very close friend of the family, it's better to decline. If you do attend, you may find that saké or other types of alcohol are served. Keep your alcohol consumption light or moderate; it is absolutely inappropriate to overindulge.

Appropriate attire for a wake or funeral is a black or dark suit with a black tie for men. Notice that this is the same dress code as for a wedding, with the exception of a dark tie instead of a white one. Women can wear a dark dress or suit.

You will be given a packet of salt when you leave. Custom calls for you to have this salt sprinkled on you before you enter your home. Salt has been used for purification rituals for centuries. In this instance, it is intended to remove all traces of death from you before entering your own home.

SEXUAL ORIENTATION

Japan is one the most progressive of the Asian countries when it comes to tolerance for differences in sexual orientation. Same-sex couples, however, are subject to the same unwritten social rules as heterosexual couples when it comes to public behavior. Public displays of affection are inappropriate for any couple, regardless of sexual orientation.

Although there are no laws against homosexuality, same-sex marriages or partnerships are not legally recognized. Therefore, a same-sex partner will have no access to his or her partner's benefits, such as insurance or death benefits. There is little legislative or judicial precedent concerning sexual orientation, such as employment discrimination. However, transgender rights have been recognized to the extent that sex-change operations have been designated as acceptable medical procedures that can be legally performed in Japan.

You shouldn't experience any problems traveling as a same-sex couple, but discretion is a good idea when traveling in rural areas. As in most places, you will find a more active gay and lesbian scene in Tokyo and other larger cities than you will in smaller towns.

International Friends is a nonprofit support and social group for those with alternative lifestyles in Tokyo. You can find contact information in the phone book or by visiting their site at http://www.geocities.com/WestHollywood/4248/index.html.

FOOD

To the uninitiated, Japanese food equals sushi. The Japanese certainly eat sushi, but in truth Japanese cuisine is much more varied. You can find almost anything you desire in Japan, international fare included. There are entire books devoted to the topic of Japanese food, so it is obviously impossible to create an all-inclusive guide to Japanese cuisine in a few short paragraphs. This section is intended to be a brief overview of some of the common components of the Japanese diet. Hopefully it will entice you to explore the wonderful variety of food you will have access to in Japan.

The Japanese take food very seriously, both in restaurants and at home. Fresh ingredients are preferred and the presentation of the food is just as important as the food itself. Even vegetables are not tossed onto the plate, denuded, and cut into rough sticks; they are cut into decorative shapes or given scalloped edges before being carefully arranged on the plate. Similar care goes into the preparation of the food as well, and the result is a gastronomical delight. Even if you've visited every Japanese restaurant between London and Los Angeles, you are likely to find that Japanese food served at its origin tastes different—and better—than what is served abroad.

Sushi is what immediately comes to mind when one thinks of Japanese food. There are two main kinds of sushi: *nigiri*, fish rolled in rice, and *maki*, fish rolled in seaweed. Other options include *oshi*, fish molded around rice, and *inari*, rice tucked into fried tofu. Sashimi is the fish without the rice. If your fingers are cramped and you're feeling faint with hunger because you can't seem to get the food from the plate to your mouth using chopsticks, pop in for some sushi—it's perfectly acceptable to eat it with your fingers!

Sushi can be ordered à la carte or as part of a mixed platter. Note that when ordered à la carte, the portion is usually two pieces of sushi, although the price listed may be for one piece. Sushi at a good restaurant can be quite pricey, but there are other alternatives, such as less expensive restaurants that send freshly-prepared sushi out on a conveyor belt. Plates are color coded by price and diners simply grab what they want and are charged according to the number and color of the plates they accumulate. To go along with your sushi, you need to know about *wasabi* (a green horseradish paste that is very spicy), *shōyu* (soy sauce), and *gari* (slices of pickled ginger). The *wasabi* may be inside certain types of sushi. The *shōyu* will be in a bottle; pour a small amount into the small bowl at your place and dip your sushi in it if you wish. The *gari* is meant to refresh the palate before trying a different type of sushi.

If the idea of eating raw fish is too much for you, try tempura first. Tempura is pieces of prawns, fish, or vegetable dipped into a batter and fried. You will get a bowl of *ten-tsuyu*, a brown sauce, and a plate of *daikon*, grated radish. Mix the *daikon* into the *ten-tsuyu* and dip your tempura into the mixture. You can order tempura à la carte or as a platter including rice, miso soup, and Japanese pickles.

Soba and *udon* are both types of Japanese noodles. *Soba* are buckwheat noodles and are thin and brown; *udon* are wheat noodles and are thick and white. Noodles can be served hot or cold. Some of the more popular dishes are *kake-soba*, *soba* or *udon* in a hot broth, and *mori-soba*, a dish of noodles with a cold broth for dipping. You may never break your kids of this habit when you move back home, but don't forget that you're expected to slurp your soup.

Unagi (eel) is another popular dish, though not a cheap one. *Unagi* is generally brushed with a soy and sake sauce and grilled. For the adventurous, there is *fugu* (blowfish). Eating this fish can be literally fatal if it's not prepared properly, since the fish has a poisonous gland that must be removed without being ruptured. The fish itself isn't particularly tasty and falls in the general "tastes like chicken" category, so the biggest pleasure in eating it comes from the thrill of danger.

When you're ready for some nice deep-fried food, you can try *tonkatsu*, a breaded, deep-fried pork cutlet. Or raise your cholesterol with *kushiage* or *kushikatsu*, deep-fried skewers of seafood, meat, or vegetables.

Dining Out

Japan offers a huge selection of fare, from Japanese haute cuisine to fast-food restaurants. In major cities you will be able to find restaurants specializing in just about anything, including Indian, Chinese, Italian, and French cuisine.

You will see short curtains hung above the door of many restaurants. These *noren* act as an open/closed sign: The curtain is hung out when the restaurant is open and taken back inside when it closes.

Menus are often in Japanese only. If you can't read the menu, you can ask your companions or the waiter or waitress to suggest something. Many restaurants have plastic displays of their dishes in the window to entice customers; it's okay to drag the waiter or waitress to the display to point out what you want, if necessary.

You will find that Japanese waiters and waitresses are generally very attentive, but if you do need to beckon a server, raise your hand, catch his or her eye and say "*onegaishimasu*" ("please").

At the end of the meal, your bill will be laid on your table. Take it to the cashier at the front of the restaurant to pay. Do not leave money to pay for the meal on your table. A tip is not expected.

Coworkers eating lunch together or friends sharing a cup of tea usually split the bill, but you will often find yourself in situations where you are either the guest or the host. If someone is hosting, such as at a business dinner, it's common for the host to discreetly excuse himself or herself toward the end of the meal to pay. This is an especially useful trick for women who find that male dinner companions are unwilling to let them pay, even when it's a business meal.

Remember that cash is the preferred way of paying in Japan, so the restaurant may not accept credit cards—be sure you have enough cash to pay for the meal.

Types of Restaurants

The following is by no means an exhaustive list; it's meant to be a quick introduction to some of the common types of restaurants you will see in Japan. There are also many specialty restaurants that defy categorization. As is true almost everywhere nowadays, Western fast-food restaurants have insinuated themselves into virtually every street corner, so you can easily satisfy that craving for a burger and fries, fried chicken, or pizza. You'll also see Japanese fast-food restaurants such as Yoshinoya, Mos Burger, and Ten'ya interspersed among the golden arches.

Shokudō

These are the most common types of restaurants, inexpensive and serving a variety of both Japanese and Western food. *Shokudō* gener-

ally offer a fixed-price meal (*teishoku*) that includes a meat or fish main dish, rice, miso, shredded cabbage, and pickles. *Teishoku* are alternately called *ranchi setto* or *kōsu*.

Izakaya

Izakaya are casual, usually inexpensive places where you can get a bite to eat while you drink your beer or sake. You can sit at the bar or a table or on the *tatami* mats and select from a wide variety of relatively simple fare.

Teishokuya

Teishokuya are very inexpensive restaurants where you get your dishes a la carte. Many are self-service cafeteria style, where you select the items you want from the rack and pay the cashier. In others you buy tickets for what you want and give them to the server who comes to your table. *Teishokuya* are often filled with students, since the price is right for a student budget.

Bentōya

This is Japanese take-out. You can select from a variety of *bentō* (hot or cold boxed lunches) to take with you if you are in a hurry or want to eat at home but just don't feel like making your own dinner.

Robatayaki

If you want entertainment with your dinner, try a *robatayaki*. You will sit at the counter with a variety of fresh food on display on a bed of ice. Diners point to what they want and the chefs toss it onto the grill with much flourishing of knives and utensils. Eating at a *robatayaki* can be more expensive than eating at the aforementioned places, but it can be worth it just for the entertainment value. Most *robatayaki* go to great lengths to create a rustic atmosphere in keeping with the theme of cooking on an open hearth.

Dining Etiquette

When you dine with colleagues or friends, you'll want to be sure your table manners are up to par. Following are a few guidelines, but it's also a good idea to observe your fellow diners and follow their lead.

Seating arrangements are very important. In restaurants, as in a private home, the guest of honor is seated in front of the *takonoma* or, if there is none, in the seat furthest from the door or with the best view.

After you are seated at your table in a restaurant, you will be given an *oshibori* (hot towel). Use it to wipe your hands, then roll it up and place it on the table next to you. Never use the *oshibori* for your face.

The guests are served by rank, starting with the highest ranking person. If there is a guest of honor, wait for him or her start eating before you dig in. If there is no guest of honor, wait until everyone has been served. It's customary to say "*Itadakimasu*" (literally, "I will receive," but meant more as "Thanks to the host/hostess/cook") before beginning to eat.

Try to take at least a little taste of each dish you are offered. If your plate is empty, it will be refilled, so when you are full, leave a little bit of food on your plate.

You will hear people slurping their soup; this is perfectly acceptable in Japan. Hold soup bowls and small dishes with dipping sauce up close to your mouth to avoid dripping.

If you are served tea in a teacup with a lid, remove the lid and place it top-down on the table next to your cup. Use both hands to hold the cup, one hand on the bottom and one hand holding the side.

It's impolite to grab the pot or bottle for a refill, so always let someone else fill your cup or glass. Keep an eye on your neighbors' glasses, too, so you can keep them filled.

When you are done with your meal, it's polite to say "*Gochisōsama*" (loosely translated as "The food was delicious") to your host. If you're in a restaurant, you'll also use this phrase when you pay the bill or, if you are the guest, you'll say it to your host when you leave the restaurant.

Chopsticks Dos and Don'ts

When you are ready to put your chopsticks (*hashi*) down, place them side by side on the table with the tips pointing to the left and resting on the *hashioki* (chopstick rest). Food is generally served individually, but if there is a common plate, reverse your chopsticks to serve yourself; the end you eat with shouldn't be put into food that others will eat.

There are a couple of things to avoid doing with your chopsticks. Don't spear food with your chopsticks or use them to pull a dish toward you.

Chopsticks should never be stuck upright in your rice, since this is reminiscent of how rice is offered to ancestors in Buddhist rituals. Don't use them to punctuate your sentences or wave them in the air. Don't use your chopsticks to cut the food on your plate. If you encounter a piece of meat or vegetable too large to just pop into your mouth, hold it with the chopsticks and take a bite.

HEALTH AND SAFETY

High quality health care is available throughout Japan, but it comes at a price. It is mandatory for everyone to be covered by health insurance, either through his or her employer or through the national insurance program. National insurance is designed to provide health insurance for self-employed people, those who work for smaller companies that do not have an employee plan, and people who are otherwise not covered by an employee plan. Most expatriates find that their companies have an insurance plan in which all employees are enrolled. Your monthly premium is based on your income; you pay half of the premium and the company pays for half.

If you go to the doctor or hospital, you will pay 10% to 30% of the bill when you present your insurance card, depending on what type of insurance you have and whether it's a doctor's visit, outpatient treatment, or hospitalization. You can check with your employer's benefits administrator for the details of your plan and availability of additional insurance.

Ask your colleagues or friends to recommend a doctor or dentist. If you don't speak Japanese, it will be important to find medical professionals who speak English; other expatriates can be a valuable source of information. You can also contact the Tourist Information Center for lists of English-speaking doctors in large cities.

Tap water is safe to drink throughout Japan. Likewise, there are few problems with eating raw vegetables or fish (i.e., sushi or sashimi), other than the usual consequences of a change of diet.

Earthquakes

Earthquakes are not infrequent occurrences in Japan. If you're from California, this may be par for the course for you, but if you are unfamiliar with what to do in the event of an earthquake, here are a few tips.

Turn off all appliances, especially gas ones, immediately. Open the doors to your apartment or house to ensure that they don't get stuck closed. If you're in a high-rise building, avoid the elevator and use the stairs instead. In most cases, its preferable to stay indoors; you may be hit by falling glass or other items if you rush outside. Crouch in a doorway or under a sturdy desk to avoid being hit by falling objects. If you're at a beach, evacuate immediately; tsunamis or tidal waves can be caused by earthquakes. If you are driving, pull over immediately. Emergency personnel have plans in place to enforce traffic restrictions in the event of a major earthquake.

CRIME AND LEGAL ISSUES

Japan is quite a safe country, with a crime rate about one-fifth that of the U.S. Violent crime is rare and even muggings are almost unheard of, but, just like anywhere in the world, it's wise to take precautions against pickpockets in major cities. Although it's generally safe to travel on trains and subways at all times, women should be aware of *chikan*, men who take advantage of crowded rush hours to grope women or who expose themselves on dark streets.

Some things that will get you into serious trouble in Japan are drunk driving or possession of drugs, firearms, or pornography. If you misstep and find yourself on the wrong side of the law, know that the police can hold you for up to three days without charging you, and they are not obligated to allow you a phone call. They must, however, allow you to have an interpreter.

Emergency Numbers

Police: 110
Fire and ambulance: 119

Remember that if you need to make an emergency call from a public phone, the call is free. Simply press the red emergency button, then dial the appropriate emergency number.

POST OFFICE

Postal service in Japan is quite efficient and reliable. You can address your letters using *rōmaji* (roman characters), even for mail being sent within Japan, but be sure to write clearly; it's wise to print the characters, avoiding cursive script.

Local post offices are generally open from 9:00 AM to 5:00 PM Monday through Friday. The main post office in the *ku* (ward) is usually open from 9:00 AM to 7:00 PM on weekdays and from 9:00 AM to 3:00 PM on Saturdays. The main post office in larger cities may have one window that is open 24 hours a day every day of the week. You can find a post office by looking for a white sign with a red symbol resembling a *T* with an extra bar on top.

Postal rates in Japan are fairly high, with postcards costing ¥70 for international delivery and a 10-gram letter to North America costing ¥110. For domestic mail, you will pay ¥80 for letters up to 25 grams and ¥50 for a postcard. Extra weight or odd-sized envelopes will cost a bit more.

International business mail is available for mail sent to foreign destinations as well as for in-country business mail. Items sent by international business mail to major cities, such as New York or London, will be delivered quickly, usually in three days or less.

If you need to post a letter while you're out and about, look for red mailboxes for ordinary mail or blue ones for special delivery post. They will be clearly marked with the post office symbol described above. There are usually two slots. One slot is for local delivery and will be marked *Tokyo-to-nai* (or similar for other cities). The other slot is for other areas and will be marked *sonota no chiiki*.

Special mail services such as registered mail, insured mail, or delivery receipt are available when you take your letter or package to the post office. The extra charge for these services will depend on the size and weight of the item being sent and its destination.

It's best to take international mail directly to the post office; international mail dropped in a mailbox will take extra time to process. Note that you cannot leave a letter in your home mailbox for pickup; this service does not exist in Japan.

If you receive a package, but are not home when it's delivered, a second delivery attempt will be made between 5:00 and 9:00 PM. If you are not there when the second attempt is made, the mail carrier will leave a non-delivery notice. You can either mail the non-delivery notice card back to the post office specifying the date and location (e.g., at a neighbor's) when the package can be redelivered or you can pick up the package at the post office, where it will be held for seven days. You will need to bring the non-delivery notice and identification with you when you pick up the package.

For detailed postal rate charts, visit the English-language postal service Web site at http://www.post.yusei.go.jp/new-eng/. The Web site also includes diagrams of forms you might see or use with English translations.

Private delivery companies, such as DHL and Federal Express have offices throughout Japan for domestic and international packages.

TIPPING

Tipping is practically nonexistent in Japan. People in service-oriented jobs, such as restaurant and hotel staff, consider themselves professionals and do not expect to receive extra money for doing their jobs well. A tip offered is almost certain to be refused and may even be viewed as an insult.

The single exception to the tipping rule is taxis. While drivers are not tipped for simply dropping you off at your destination, they will gladly accept a small tip when they provide extra services, such as carrying your luggage to your door.

BUSINESS
ENVIRONMENT

Before beginning to do business in Japan, it will be helpful to learn about the Japanese business environment. This chapter will acquaint you with the basics of business in Japan. However, it is important to note that, as elsewhere, things are changing in Japan. Therefore, this chapter seeks to acquaint you with both the traditional ways of doing business and recent modifications to these traditions.

COMPANY VALUES

Much of Japan's economic success is the result of great company loyalty, a level of commitment by employees who toil and sweat long hours for the benefit of their companies. Of course, company loyalty is a symbiotic relationship between employer and employee. In return for their loyalty, employees were taken into the "family" of the company, where they were assured lifetime employment, steady promotions, and salary increases until they reached retirement and their company pension. The company became much more than an employer along the way, often providing many of the basic necessities of life, such as housing, as well as social and cultural events.

The company strives to create loyalty in many ways, and, indeed, many typical Japanese business practices breed loyalty. For example, a Japanese student may seek assistance from his university's alumni in finding a job, and he may live in the company dormitory for several years. He might even meet and marry a girl from the office. He is brought into the fold as part of a *dōkikai,* or same-year group, and together they participate in activities and outings that teach them how to become part of the company family and cement their personal bonds. The structure of a Japanese company means that this group of people will advance through their careers together, leading to a strong bond between members of the same *dōkikai.*

In addition to company loyalty, there is individual loyalty. A young Japanese salaryman has many personal ties to individuals in the company. For example, he has an important obligation to the alumni of his university and will strive to make sure he does nothing to cause them shame. He has similar obligations to his coworkers and to his manager, and as he works his way up the corporate ladder, he gains responsibility for those under his supervision. These are the building blocks of company loyalty.

This level of loyalty to an organization and to one's coworkers is quite the opposite of what is typically found in the U.S. Indeed, the very first encounter between an American and a Japanese businessperson illustrates this fundamental difference. The American introduces himself first, then his company: "Hi, I'm Chris Montrose from ABC Company," but the Japanese first states his company, then his own name: "*Konnichiwa. ABC no Montrose desu.*"

Company loyalty is still an integral part of Japanese business, but the "family" ties that bind companies and employees are gradually loosening for many reasons. In some cases, companies have been forced to downsize in order to remain competitive, and some have begun to adapt performance-based Western business practices to their needs. The face of the Japanese workforce has changed as well as a generation of technologically-savvy young people enter the job market. The younger generation has less patience for the traditional practices and is more open to the idea of changing jobs. It is important to stress, however, that these trends are relatively new and are not by any means widespread.

Although there is a growing trend in Japan for workers, especially white-collar workers, to change jobs, lifetime employment is far from obsolete.

COMPANY STRUCTURE

There are five basic types of business structures in Japan: sole proprietorship, commercial partnership, limited partnership, general corporation, and limited liability corporation. The following paragraphs provide a brief overview of the different types of company structures. Of course, there are advantages and disadvantages to each type of structure, such as tax treatment and the amount of personal liability one has for the company's debts. However, prior to recent reforms in capital requirements for corporations, many companies, large and small, opted to form corporations for the sole benefit of the prestige associated with corporations, prestige that partnerships and sole proprietorships simply do not carry.

Sole Proprietorship

A sole proprietorship is, of course, a business owned by one person. In a sole proprietorship, the business owner is liable for all of the business actions and debts.

Commercial Partnership (Gō-mei Gaisha)

In this type of partnership, all partners can be held personally responsible for any liabilities incurred by the partnership. Liability is unlimited and creditors are able to seize personal assets if the partnership cannot meet its obligations.

Limited Partnership (Gō-shi Gaisha)

Limited partnerships have two types of partners: general partners and limited partners. As in a commercial partnership, general partners have unlimited liability. The liability of limited partners, however, is limited to the amount of that partner's investment in the company.

General Corporation (Kabushiki Gaisha)

A general corporation shields shareholders from being held personally responsible for the company's liabilities, limiting liability of partners to the amount invested in the corporation. Current capital requirements for the formation of a general corporation are ¥10,000,000.

Limited Liability Corporation (Yūgen Gaisha)

Because the general corporation structure does not fully meet the needs of many medium and small businesses, the limited liability corporation can fill that gap, since it is easier to register and less costly to incorporate. The liability of shareholders is similar to that of a general corporation, but there are limitations on the number of shareholders the corporation can have, as well as limits on the transfer of shares. Current capital requirements for the formation of a general corporation are ¥3,000,000.

WHO'S WHO IN THE OFFICE

Rank is very much respected in Japanese organizations, so it is essential that you know with whom you are dealing. In many organizations, people, especially managers and executives, are called by their titles instead of by their names. Following are the most common.

Kaichō	Chairman
Sōdan-yaku	Advisor
Komon	Counselor
Shachō	President
Fuku Shachō	Vice President
Semmu Torishimariyaku	Senior Executive Director
Jōmu Torishimariyaku	Executive Managing Director
Torishimariyaku	Director
Buchō	Department Manager
Buchō Dairi	Deputy Department Manager
Kachō	Section Chief
Kachō Dairi	Deputy Section Chief
Kakarichō	Chief Clerk

Although the president is the top man in the company, Japanese companies usually take care of their retired executives and take advantage of their knowledge and experience. Their input is sought when major decisions are made, and their opinions usually carry a great deal of weight.

The *kaichō* (chairman) is very often a retired president who is no longer involved in the day-to-day business. Despite his retirement, the *kaichō* can be as influential as the *shachō* when it comes to making decisions.

The titles of *sōdan-yaku* (advisor) and *komon* (counselor) are often honorary ones given to retired executives. Like the chairman, advisors and counselors are usually not involved in the daily running of the business, but don't underestimate the informal clout some of these individuals have.

BUSINESS HOURS

Most businesses operate on a 9:00 AM to 5:00 PM schedule, although, as you will read below, there are probably many employees still in the office several hours into the evening. Retail stores are usually open later than offices, usually until about 6:30 or 7:00, while banks tend to close around 3:00.

Japanese white-collar workers, often called salarymen, generally arrive at the office about 10 to 15 minutes before office hours begin so they can prepare for the day, and they almost never leave before their manager.

THE JAPANESE WORK WEEK AND BENEFITS

According to Japanese law, the work week is 40 hours for most workers, 44 for employees of some small businesses. However, if you take a count of the workers rushing into their offices at 9:00 in the morning and compare it to the number of people going home at 5:00, the numbers just wouldn't add up. That's because most salarymen at all levels work a lot of overtime, and many routinely stay in their offices until 8:00 PM or later.

Salaries are paid monthly, but the annual salary is usually divided into 18 parts. The employee then receives the equivalent of two months' salary in June and four months' in December as a year-end bonus. The bonus amount does depend on the financial performance of the company, and more and more companies are also considering job performance in their bonus calculations. Paid overtime is common for non-managerial staff, but is determined by contract.

The typical Japanese worker is on a probationary period for the first six months with a new employer. Once that time is up, the employee usually gets 10 days of paid vacation for the first year, with a day added for each subsequent year of service, up to 20 total days of vacation. Many Japanese, especially older workers, are reluctant to take their vacation days because they feel that their commitment to their work team is more important or because they feel that they might miss something important if they are gone for too long. In recent years, the government has teamed up with businesses to encourage employees to take all of their vacation days. Not surprisingly, the younger generation of employees has fewer reservations about taking full advantage of their allotted vacation time.

In addition to annual vacation days, Japan has 14 national holidays a year. Many companies also give employees one or two extra summer holidays in August; in manufacturing industries, the plant may close for an entire week in mid-August.

Compensation in most companies is equitably distributed across levels, a practice made possible by a system that brings everyone in at the bottom level after the university and provides slow but steady promotion.

Many Japanese salarymen live quite some distance from their offices. For example, an employee of a Tokyo-based company may live in a suburb 1 1/2 to 2 hours away. It's common, therefore, for employers to pay all or part of the cost of commuting to work, either by buying the employee's monthly commuter pass or by reimbursing the employee for travel expenses.

Japanese workers, like their counterparts around the world, come home with a paycheck that is substantially less than their gross salary. Deductions are made for health insurance, pension plans, labor insurance and, of course, tax.

There are three options for health insurance: *Shakai hoken* (Employees' Health Insurance), *Kokumin kenkō hoken* (National Health Insurance), or private insurance. Most employers enroll their employees in an insurance program in which the cost of the premium is shared equally by the employee and the employer. Those who are self-employed or whose employers do not offer an insurance plan can enroll in the national health insurance program, administered by local wards and municipalities. The cost of the premiums is determined by a formula based on the amount of the individual's local tax payment. Some companies provide insurance through a private company; this is especially true in foreign companies. The amount of the premiums varies according to the insurance company's policy.

Pension plans are available, as well, although many expatriates find that the benefits are minimal if they are scheduled to stay in Japan for only a short period of time. *Kōsei nenkin* (Employees' Pension) are plans offered by the company. If a company offers a pension plan, participation is usually mandatory for all employees. The amount of the premium is calculated based on the employee's annual salary and the cost is shared equally by the company and the employee. All people between the ages of 20 and 59 are eligible to participate in the *Kokumin nenkin* (National Pension Plan). The catch, though, is that in order to collect pension benefits, one must pay into the program for at least 25 years, a stretch of time that is not applicable in most expatriate assignments. This plan is locally administered and the premium is a set monthly amount.

OFFICE SPACE

Contrary to the American desire for a private workspace, the Japanese tend to view cubicles and offices as isolating and not conducive to teamwork. But just as American workspaces reflect the values of individuality and an independent work style, so too does the Japanese open workspace reflect Japanese values.

In a typical, traditional Japanese office, the lowest ranking employees, usually the office ladies (see the section on office ladies in this chapter), sit closest to the door and the highest ranking managers have their desks the furthest into the office. Employees sit together in several small islands, their desks facing one another. At the head of the island, facing the group, is the desk of the *kakaricho*, or chief. Overlooking these are the desks of the *kachō*, or section chief, and *buchō*, or department chief. With this arrangement, teams sit together and can work together to complete their assignments, eliminating much of the need for status meetings or reports, while managers are on hand to provide support and input as needed.

Depending on the nature of the business, two or more people may share a computer terminal or even a telephone.

WA (HARMONY)

Harmony is a goal not just in the business environment, but in all aspects of life. Don't confuse *wa* with peace and quiet. If you recall, the typical Japanese office is open, with most of the employees sitting in groups. No matter how quietly each person talks, the cumulative volume can get rather high.

Wa refers to harmony between two people, to harmonious relationships. It is important in Japan, where people work in teams in pursuit of one goal rather than as individuals. Disharmony at any level can have a negative impact on the entire group.

Many things contribute to *wa*. For example, the indirect communication style ensures that no one loses face and the preference for consensus in decision-making maintains goodwill at many levels. The setup of the office, too, means that the *buchō* or *kachō* is on hand to resolve any problems that might arise that disturb the harmony of the group.

DŌKIKAI (SAME YEAR GROUP)

Much of the hiring in the corporate world is done in the spring as each new class of university graduates leaves the world of academia in search of a job. There are unwritten rules governing the date when companies can start recruiting, as well as a general agreement on the salaries paid to new hires in the same industry. This creates a level playing field for all Japanese companies seeking to recruit new talent.

Regardless of which section they are assigned to, all new employees for the year are members of the same *dōkikai* and the company does all it can to create a feeling of loyalty to both the company and to one another. Most companies do many things to help all of the incoming employees get to know each other and learn to work together. Events are planned for the *dōkikai*, ranging from dinner parties to retreats. Years after the group has settled into the company, the members of the *dōkikai* continue to get together for outings, forming teams for Sports Day and for other extracurricular activities. Thus, the *dōkikai* becomes an important part of a Japanese employee's network, both professionally and personally.

As a young graduate entering a company, the members of your *dōkikai* are the people with whom you will be working with for a long time, possibly 30 years or more. Together you will rise through the ranks as you gain experience. Of course, since there are fewer positions at the top of the pyramid than at the bottom, some will rise to greater heights than others, so the members of your *dōkikai* are also the people who will be your competition when it's time for promotion.

CLIMBING THE CORPORATE LADDER

Advancement through a Japanese organization can seem excruciatingly slow to someone who is used to an organization where employees can become vice presidents after a few short years of work. Most Japanese organizations operate on a seniority system (*nenkō-joretsu*) where a salaryman's rank in the company rises with his age. A Japanese employee can expect to receive steady annual salary increases, regular reassignments, and occasional promotions. For example, he may get transferred to a new assignment or section every 3–5 years so he can gain a wide variety of experience. These are important steps in a salaryman's career, since only those who have this wide base of experience are truly in a position to rise to an important position within the company. In short, working your way up the Japanese corporate ladder is much more akin to a marathon than a sprint.

The *nenkō-joretsu* works in Japan for many reasons. It is very much in keeping with the Japanese values of respect for age and experience, and it helps foster loyalty to the company and the family atmosphere in the company. It also makes it more attractive for most people to stay at one company; after all, someone who leaves after ten years spent earning the respect of his colleagues and attaining his current position faces a new environment where he has to rebuild those relationships and the trust that he had earned over the last decade.

Obviously it is impossible to have everyone rise to very elite positions in the company—a company that did that would end up with more people at the top than at the bottom. Only a few employees can stay on the path that leads to the executive office. Other employees who perform well will end up with smaller but well respected titles, such as *buchō*. Even the employees who don't live up to expectations stay on at the company. They receive their annual salary raise like everyone else, but are eventually assigned some nebulous, relatively meaningless title and have very little real responsibility.

Because the trail to the top is predictable, most people will know within a few years where they are likely to end up in the long run. Particular attention is paid to transfers and reassignment, as they are indicative of where the path is leading. For example, a lateral transfer to the home office in Tokyo is most definitely an upward move, while a transfer from the home office to a small, out-of-the-way branch office is usually seen as a step down, even if the position itself is higher.

THE JAPANESE WORKFORCE

The Japanese workforce has both blue-collar workers and white-collar workers, but it is the Japanese salaryman, the white-collar worker, who is largely responsible for Japan's post-war economic boom. They have become especially important as Japan has moved from heavy manufacturing to focus more and more on technology and service-oriented industries.

The term "salaryman" is used to refer to the workers who fill Japan's offices in every industry from finance to manufacturing. Of course, other employees can be salaried, such as retail sales staff and even plant workers, but this term is reserved for the office worker. Salarymen usually have a college education and most are hired by the company when they graduate; many will stay with the same company until they retire.

The Japanese Salaryman

Commuter trains are packed every morning with Japanese salary-men rushing off to work. The salaryman is generally in "uniform," with his dark blue or gray suit (black suits are only worn at funerals) and black shoes, his white shirt and conservative tie. His hair is short and neat and he carries the accoutrements of his occupation: an attaché case or small bag in one hand and a newspaper, comic book, or novel to keep him occupied during the long commute.

The salaryman goes to the office Monday through Friday and sometimes on Saturday as he pursues his promotions. Because most people live in the suburbs of the largest cities, many salarymen face a commute that takes up to two hours each way. He rises early in the morning, probably before his children get up, so he can be in the office by 9:00 or 9:30—or even 8:00 if he has designs on the top spots in the company. He works through the morning until it is time for lunch at noon. During his lunch hour, he eats at a nearby restaurant or stops at a noodle shop for *tachigui soba* (noodles eaten while standing). His wife might pack him an *aisai bentō* ("devoted wife" boxed lunch), which he eats at his desk. He may enjoy his full lunch hour by taking a short jog or sitting and talking with his friends, or he may go straight back to work. He spends the afternoon working, often staying in the office until 8:00 PM. If he wants to advance, he may stay even later, putting in a few hours of study each day. Thus the salaryman arrives home, dead tired, somewhere between 10:00 PM and 1:00 AM, after his children have gone to bed.

In this scenario, of course, the salaryman has little time to spend with his family, and, indeed, even some of his spare time can be taken up by activities related to his job. For example, his section may organize a group trip or activity. These are difficult to decline and very often the families of the employees are not invited, since the goal of the activity is to strengthen personal ties within the group. The salaryman might also play on the company's baseball team or participate in another company-sponsored club. And, of course, when your boss invites you to play golf, you'd be a fool to decline.

Solo transfers, too, are not uncommon. This describes a tempo-

rary transfer to another city while the family stays behind. The
salaryman may end up traveling several hours to visit his family on
weekends.

Needless to say, the life of many salarymen leaves little time to
spend with one's family or to simply relax. Stress is a very real problem for salarymen and health problems abound, including ulcers,
stomach problems, and high blood pressure.

WOMEN IN BUSINESS

More and more Japanese women are entering the workforce. In the
past, most women took a job only as a stopgap until they got married—
or even as a way to find a suitable husband. While this trend has by no
means disappeared, women today enter the workforce for a variety of
reasons. Some women work because they prefer the lifestyle they can
have on two family salaries while some women enjoy the stimulation
of a career, whether or not they really need the additional salary.

The issue of gender equality is one that is evolving in Japan. According to a law enacted in 1986, men and women should be treated
equally at work. However, as is often the case, this has not resulted in
overnight change. In fact, like most changes in Japan, the inclusion
of women in the workplace is a slow, gradual process.

Many Americans take a critical view of this plodding approach to
creating equality for women without recognizing the inherent differences in the cultures and social norms. That is, the American culture
usually forces change through the courts. Change is brought about
more subtly in Japan, with government providing leadership in the
form of education: teaching employers how to bring their hiring and
work practices in line with legislation, and teaching women how to
integrate into a male-dominated workforce. Great strides have been
made in both countries over the last decade, each approaching the
issue in different ways. Still, neither Japan nor the U.S. has reached
full gender equality.

In Japan, women often get paid less than their male counterparts
for doing the same job, and they are usually not offered the same range

of opportunity. In fact, many Western companies have taken advantage of this imbalance, recognizing the wellspring of latent talent sitting dormant in many Japanese offices and offering women more opportunities for career growth, often at more competitive salaries.

Although women have advanced their position toward equality in the workplace, societal norms have not yet caught up. Therefore, women are still the ones who take most of the responsibility for running the home, raising the children, and caring for aging parents. Taking care of aging parents is traditionally the responsibility of the oldest son, but in reality it falls mainly to his wife. If a woman has no brother, she may find herself with two sets of parents to care for: her husband's and her own.

Office Ladies

Office ladies, or OL, used to be the typical example of a woman who takes a low-level job after high school only until she finds a husband

and marries. The duties of the OL were to serve tea or coffee and perform other small tasks. However, they also performed essential duties in the organization, such as acting as gatekeepers and helping establish and maintain harmonious relationships in the office.

Although the OL is still a common fixture in Japanese companies, more and more women today have elected to stay in the workforce as professional women. These women are finding their niche in the organization, rather than doing general office tasks, and they are moving up in the company. More women are also attending university and are entering the workforce on an equal educational footing with men, and they have the same expectations for advancement to managerial positions.

Tips for Women in Business

Western women often find the Japanese business environment extremely difficult to handle. A woman may notice that the automatic assumption in a male-dominated office is that she is the subordinate or assistant. Many men will have the tendency to direct their comments and questions to her male colleagues and more or less ignore her. However, being a foreigner can also have its advantages, and she will probably also discover that her Japanese contacts and colleagues accord her a level of respect that they would not necessarily offer a Japanese woman in a similar position.

The best way to be effective as a foreign businesswoman in Japan is to be competent and professional. A woman traveling to Japan on business trips or meeting a client for the first time can coach her team ahead of time so that the proper protocol is followed, making it clear that she is in a position of authority.

A woman working in Japan who suspects that she is being discriminated against or treated unfairly by male colleagues will be better served to approach things circumspectly rather than reacting overtly and publicly to suspected slights, which will probably only serve to damage relationships. She can first check her own perceptions with a female colleague to see if she is understanding the situation correctly, and she can approach a manager she trusts for intervention. If issues of discrimination are not resolved by the company, a woman can take her concerns to the local labor office.

By the Way . . .

Women should be prepared to be asked very personal questions, such as if they are married or have a boyfriend, or why they are not married.

LABOR UNIONS

Labor unions in Japan are organized by industry; overall, fewer than 30% of workers belong to a union. The union's main role is to negotiate annual salary and bonus increases, but they have increasingly begun to focus on quality of life issues as well.

Annual wage negotiations generally take place in March or April and strikes occasionally occur if an agreement cannot be reached. Strikes are uncommon, but not unheard of. The negotiations that everyone in the country keeps their eyes on are in the transportation industry. A transit strike (*shuntō,* or spring offense) has the potential to throw a huge monkey wrench into the well-oiled machinery of the transportation system, leaving millions of people scrambling to get to work.

TODAY'S JAPAN

Japan, like all countries, is not static, vacuum-sealed in time. Much has changed in recent decades, and will continue to change. Recent years have seen increased layoffs and early retirement packages, perhaps signaling the beginning of the end for the tradition of lifetime employment. Younger employees, too, sensing growing instability in the job markets, are less satisfied staying in one place. As a result, job changes, once virtually unheard of, are on the rise.

As each generation replaces the previous one, new ideas are explored, while old ideas and traditions are questioned. Today's young workers are of a generation that has never seen war, a generation raised on technology. Their values are not always the same as those of their elders and they are often chafed by the traditions of their elders. None of this means that there is an overt cultural revolution happening in Japan, but it does mean that as time moves on, so too does the Japanese culture. The generation gap is already evident in the increasing individuality of younger workers and their willingness to separate themselves from the company on many levels. Ideals of devotion to the company are being replaced by desire to spend more time with one's family, to leave the office at 6:00 or 7:00 instead of 10:00 or 11:00, and to take full advantage of vacations and other leisure time. In other words, younger employees are gradually moving away from making the company the center of their lives.

These trends have led to increasing incorporation of some Western business practices being melded with traditional Japanese practices. They have also forced young, educated Japanese men and women to look outside of Japan for the possibility of better career opportunities, creating a potentially dangerous drain on the pool of talent in Japan.

SEVEN

BUSINESS STEP-BY-STEP

Now that we've taken a look at the overall structure and atmosphere of business in Japan, let's take a look at the specifics.

INTRODUCTIONS AND FIRST MEETINGS

Let's say you feel like you are ready to enter the Japanese market, but you have no contacts, so you figure you'll just hop on a plane to Tokyo, grab the local yellow pages, and start making calls. That may work in some countries, but if you try it in Japan, you might as well just take that wad of money you are about to spend and toss it in the garbage can.

Introductions are essential to get your foot in the door in Japan. It is trust, not contracts, that build the foundation of a business relationship, and this is not something you can establish during a phone call. For this reason, an introduction from a mutual friend or business associate lends a sort of legitimacy to your first meeting. In other words, when a coworker introduces you to a client, a small piece of their relationship is transferred to you.

In an ideal world, you will have a personal introduction, during which your friend or colleague is present to formally introduce you to his contact. However, if that is not possible, your colleague can pave the way by speaking to his contact on your behalf, essentially asking him to meet with you. Alternatively, your colleague can provide a written letter of introduction. Although personal introductions are preferred, in a pinch you can contact your country's embassy in Japan to see if they can provide you with a letter of introduction, in effect endorsing you or your company.

Having someone act as an intermediary to help you establish contacts creates an obligation for you, too. Because your mutual friend or business associate has given you a stamp of approval, your actions will reflect on your associate. Therefore, be aware that if you do something to damage your relationship with your new acquaintance, you are at the very least denting the existing relationship between your mutual friend and your new acquaintance.

BUSINESS CARDS

With the exception of students and housewives, almost everybody in Japan carries name cards. Name cards, or *meishi*, are an important part of the Japanese business culture. Not only do they provide the necessary contact information, such as telephone and fax numbers, they are invaluable tools to help you determine your respective status to the other person, which will dictate the formality of your interaction with that person.

It's a good idea to have bilingual business cards to facilitate understanding between you and your Japanese contacts. The question of which side—English or Japanese—to present to your Japanese colleague is one with no clear-cut answer. If you know the recipient does not speak English, presenting the card Japanese side up means that

he will not need to turn the card over to read the information and consequently will avoid the embarrassing de facto admission that his English skills are nonexistent. On the other hand, if the recipient has even the most basic English skills, he will appreciate your acknowledgment of this skill in handing over your card English side up; such a gesture can also give face to the recipient. No matter what language is face up when you present the card, be sure you don't hand the card over with the text upside down for the recipient.

Traditionally, name cards or business cards were presented by holding the card at the upper corners (the corners closest to the giver) with both hands. Nowadays, it's equally common to see a one-handed presentation, with the right hand holding the upper corner. Either way, the presentation is accompanied by a bow. If the two parties already know each other—for example, if they have corresponded or spoken on the phone enough to know each other's work title—the bow reflects the relative status of the two people. If the two people do not know each other, they will generally give a small bow as they exchange cards. Once they have had a moment to read the information on the card and assess their relative status, they will bow again; this time the bow will be appropriate to each person's position.

When you receive someone's name card or business card, it's expected that you take a few moments to study it, committing the information to memory. It's also a good time to ask for the proper pronunciation of the person's name if you are unsure.

GIFT-GIVING

Occasions for giving gifts in Japan abound in business as well as social environments. It's likely that you will need to provide gifts for weddings, births, and even funerals, and you will be expected to participate in the annual gift-giving seasons of *ochūgen* and *oseibo*. The practice of giving gifts extends to your staff and coworkers, as the company in Japan is like an extended family. Gifts for other business associates, clients, and contacts are also appropriate.

Gifts are usually given at the end of a first business meeting. For example, if your company is sending a delegation to Japan to negotiate a large business deal or begin a joint project, gifts will be exchanged at the end of your first day. Be prepared, but let your Japanese hosts initiate the ceremony.

It's often very difficult to know what is appropriate to give as a business gift, especially in light of restrictions that some governments, including that of the U.S., place on the value of the gifts you can give. You can give a group gift, such as a nice coffee-table book with pictures from your hometown; if a book about your company's history exists, that would be appropriate as well. Your other option is to give individual gifts to each person in the group.

No matter what the occasion, business gifts should be of high quality, although they need not be overly expensive. It's okay to give items with a discreet company logo, but it's best to avoid the appearance of advertising. Other ideas for business gifts include high-quality liquor, such as scotch or whiskey, music, or golf balls, depending on what you know about your Japanese colleagues. Once you have established business relationships, you may wish to bring small gifts when you visit. If you are living in Japan, you could bring a gift when you return from a trip home or from a business trip. Appropriate gifts should be based on your colleague's or client's preferences, such as books or a toy for his child, or a souvenir tee from a famous golf course for the avid golfer.

You will also encounter the tradition of *omiyage*. It's customary for coworkers to give someone going on a trip, especially a trip abroad, a small amount of money to be spent on an *omiyage*, or memento of the trip that can be brought back and shared with others in a sort of show-and-tell fashion. This kindness is often returned in the form of a box of candy or other treat brought back to the office for coworkers to share.

Remember, too, that the presentation of the gift is as important as the gift itself. You can refer to the section on gift-giving in the Living and Staying in Japan chapter for more details on wrapping and presenting gifts, as well as other notes on gift-giving, such as what items and numbers to avoid, and a list of appropriate gifts for more social occasions.

SEATING ARRANGEMENTS

Seating arrangements are very important in Japan, as they reflect the status of the individuals present. You will be well advised to become attuned to the nuances of seating, since the rules will be applicable when you are driving your boss to the airport, meeting with clients, or hosting a business dinner.

If you are the visitors, of course, you need only show up; your hosts will show you to your seats and initiate the introductions. If you are the hosts, on the other hand, it's a good idea to get as much information as you can beforehand so you can be prepared and have everything in place. The way you greet your guests and the seating arrangements for both your guests and your own team will send a message, whether you intend to or not. Therefore, it's a good investment of your time to find out who will be attending and what their relative status is, draw up a seating chart, and generally make sure you observe proper protocol.

Guests are usually seated furthest from the door. The senior person sits in the middle, flanked by the subordinates, again in descending order of status; team members wait until the senior members take their seats before sitting. This arrangement applies if two groups are sitting opposite each other. The seating chart may need to be revised if there is a focal point, such as a podium or white board being used to make a presentation. In these situations, the highest ranking person is seated next to the main focal point with his or her subordinates following in descending order.

The highest ranking person should be allowed to sit down first. The visiting group always outranks the hosting group, so the senior visitor should be the first to sit.

There is also a specific set of seating rules to follow in automobiles. If there is a driver or chauffeur, the person with the highest rank sits behind the driver. If it's necessary for three people to sit in the back seat, the seat of honor is in the middle. If a colleague is driving his own car, the front passenger seat is reserved for the senior person. The senior person should also be the first to enter and exit the vehicle, if possible.

MEETINGS

Obviously, there are meetings with all kinds of different purposes in Japan, just as there are in any business environment. Many companies in Japan have daily meetings that, to an outsider, may seem to have no purpose other than to waste time. These meetings, however, are viewed as opportunities to build rapport among staff members and relay any relevant news.

Meetings in Japan are usually formal. Don't expect to walk in, roll up your sleeves, lean back in your chair, and toss ideas around. There is often an agenda to be followed and everyone is expected to behave decorously, following protocol for seating, greeting, and addressing one another. Meetings begin with several minutes of social talk before getting down to business. Speakers are listened to courteously and are not interrupted. If you recall from the Culture chapter, the Japanese are a group-oriented culture and are indirect communicators. This makes it difficult to incorporate some Western ideas, such a brainstorming sessions or impromptu presentations, into the Japanese business environment.

If you are launching a partnership or major business deal, the purpose of the first meeting may be to create a sense of harmony and goodwill between the two groups; little real business may be accomplished. Don't expect that a decision will be made or issues will be resolved in one meeting. Most items on the agenda will reappear at several subsequent meetings before they are closed.

NEGOTIATING AND PERSUADING

When it comes to negotiations, Americans and Japanese are often on opposite sides of the table, both literally and figuratively. In Japan, building a strong relationship is more important than the minutia of detailing who will do what in a partnership. As a consequence, the Japanese do not spend a great deal of time hammering out the details of a contract. Contracts are viewed more as a starting ground, a commitment to work together rather than a list of the obligations of the parties involved. Western business people, who generally set more stock in a written contract, have actually lost opportunities because of their—in the Japanese perspective—concern for the fine print.

If you are traveling to Japan for the purpose of negotiating, expect that it will take a considerable amount of time. In fact, savvy Japanese know very well that many Western business people, especially Americans, work on a very tight schedule and allow only a day or two for negotiations. They can use this against the visitors, who may give away more than they intended because they are pressed for time.

The protocol of negotiations begins when the guests walk in the door. Body language will probably tell you immediately who is the most senior person. Introductions are generally made by a junior person; the two senior people are introduced first, then others are introduced in descending order of importance. Seating is important as well and follow the guidelines outlined in the Seating Arrangements section in this chapter.

When you are negotiating with the Japanese, whether in a formal setting or in daily matters, don't expect things to happen immediately. You will not sit down at the negotiating table and walk away with a contract at the end of the day. The Japanese tend to use the meetings as information-gathering opportunities. They will want to know about you and your company, and the details of the deal in question, but discussion will take place outside of the meeting room. It's likely that many people will have to be consulted before a decision can be made, which will take some time.

Negotiations generally start at the middle management level. The negotiation is likely to be attended by several junior staff who have the necessary technical expertise and one senior person who will oversee the process. Be sure to address your presentations and questions to the group as a whole, rather than to one person. For example, if you ask the senior person for technical details that he or she does not know, you will cause a loss of face, something you want to avoid. By the same token, if you ask the same question directly to a junior person, you may also cause a loss of face by singling him or her out and breaking the protocol of status.

RINGI SHO AND NEMAWASHI IN DECISION MAKING

The process of making decisions in Japan is markedly different from what most Americans are used to. Decisions require much discussion and checking in with others for approval. Many companies continue to use the traditional system of *ringi sho*, in which an employee puts a proposal on paper, which is subsequently circulated to everyone concerned, beginning with middle management and moving up the ladder. The document passes through many hands, and each person must indicate approval by affixing their name stamps to the document.

Of course, it would cause a loss of face if you were to write up a proposal and enter it into the *ringi sho* process if you didn't know beforehand that it would pass muster. This is where *nemawashi* comes in. *Nemawashi* is informal petitioning for your proposal. Before making an idea public, a Japanese employee will speak privately with colleagues and superiors to feel them out to see if they will support the proposal. These managers will then do a little lobbying of their own with their superiors. Once approval has been informally granted, the proposal is made public and begins the rounds of *ringi sho*. Thanks to *nemawashi*, a positive result is virtually guaranteed.

The Japanese and American decision-making methods are diametrically opposed. The Japanese system of making decisions and gaining approval is time-consuming, but, it ensures that everyone involved is fully informed and on board with the decision. Because of this, once the decision has been made, the implementation is swift. Furthermore, since more time is spent on making the decision, it's unlikely that changes will be needed once the action begins.

In contrast, is the American preference for making decisions quickly, with the assumption that things can change if new information comes to light. The decision might be made at lightning speed, but there are still innumerable people who have to be told and convinced, so implementation can be quite sluggish and revisions are often necessary.

BUSINESS ENTERTAINING

Entertaining is an important part of establishing relationships in Japan. In fact, many people claim that the real business in Japan is done over dinner or on the golf course. It is a chance to get to know one another outside of the office and develop a personal side to business ties, nurturing the business relationship.

If you are engaged in a formal business deal, such as a joint venture negotiation, your Japanese hosts may have a banquet in your honor. If you are making a routine visit or are working in Japan, there will be numerous opportunities to go out for drinks with your colleagues after work. For those who have close contact with clients, there is often quite a large expense account for entertaining them.

Business entertaining is usually done in restaurants, not in homes. For more formal business matters, there will be a banquet with many courses, toasts, and gifts. Spouses are not generally included at these affairs, but a visitor's spouse is sometimes invited if she or he is along on the trip. At these occasions, you will want to put your best foot forward by displaying proper manners, so please refer to the various sections that address etiquette in the Living and Staying in Japan chapter.

Like gift-giving, the hosting of business entertainment should be reciprocated. For example, if your Japanese hosts have a banquet in your honor while you are visiting, you should try to plan a dinner for your hosts while you are there. Of course, if the Japanese will be making a return visit to your home country, it's fine to wait until they visit you to host a dinner for them.

It's common for salarymen to get together with coworkers for drinks. They are often seen in karaoke bars as well. Most people tend to go out in small groups and stick together. The groups generally don't mix, so going to a bar after work isn't the best way to meet new people.

Whatever form your business entertaining takes, it's important to remember that your presentation and behavior after hours is as important as it is during business hours. If you are the host, you will make a good impression by selecting a prestigious restaurant. If you are the guest, you should make every effort to participate by making toasts and, yes, even taking the stage to belt out an Elvis tune, if necessary.

HIRING, FIRING, AND ADVANCEMENT

The system of hiring new employees follows a prescribed path. New employees join the company once a year in April, immediately following graduation from university or high school. For university students, however, the process begins well before April. Universities

work closely with companies to set the ground rules about the dates that recruiting can begin. This set of unwritten rules is to ensure fairness for all companies and all students. Many companies have an almost exclusive arrangement with a specific university when it comes to recruiting. Therefore, a high school student who has his or her sights set on a particular company would be well advised to attend the school where that company does most of its recruiting. In fact, it's not uncommon to find that the overwhelming majority of employees in a company all went to the same university.

In the middle of the year, companies begin screening for new hires. The criteria for hiring are based partly on scholastic achievement and partly on the perceived fit of the student with the company. After all, if the intention is to keep the employee for the duration of his or her working life, it behooves both parties to make sure that they are compatible. If a candidate is extremely lucky, he or she is recruited by a company without having to apply. This can happen if a student has good connections. For example, if your uncle works at a company or if a professor who has taken an interest in you has ties to a company, that company may approach you with a job offer.

Employees are almost always hired into entry-level positions. The job description for a new employee amounts to adopting the traits of a sponge. The Japanese company expects to train their employees in all facets of the business, so a new employee's first years will probably be spent moving from department to department every three to four months in order to learn the scope of the business and get a good macro picture of what the company does and how. The employee may also receive instruction on things that may appear outside the scope of business, but that Japanese companies consider very important, such as proper etiquette and language skills, so that the employee's interaction with clients and colleagues reflects well on the company.

An employee's career path in a Japanese company is well prescribed. The large group of new hires begins as a class, called a *dōkikai*, they also rise through the ranks at about the same pace. It is not common to give one person seniority over people from his own class; the class will eventually disperse, with one person becoming a supervisor in one department while another gets a similar position in a different division. However, members of one class generally remain on par with one another, and because they have spent several years together as new recruits, they maintain a bond that strengthens the ties of the company.

Firing is a rarity in a Japanese company. It would be foolhardy to think that every single individual hired by a company anywhere will be a stellar performer. In Japan, as everywhere else, some employees simply do not perform up to par. However, a Japanese company is unlikely to fire an employee who is not doing well. He will even receive regular raises and new titles, and he will be given an office at the outside of the building, one with windows. An American walking into the office might assume that such a fellow holds a position of importance. After all, he has all of the signs of success one needs in a U.S. company—a fancy title and an office with a window. By moving the employee into this office, however, the Japanese company has essentially moved him out of the mainstream, into a job where he can do no real harm. That office with the windows that you covet is saying that its occupant has nothing better to do than gaze out the window. He has been removed from the heart of the office, where all the action is.

This may seem odd to you, not to mention a waste of money. However, the Japanese company must weigh the monetary cost of keeping some dead weight against the cost in lost morale and loyalty of its other employees if it were to fire people. In virtually every case, the intangible cost is higher than the tangible.

It is important to note that this description applies mostly to large Japanese companies. Some smaller companies, and especially foreign companies operating in Japan, do not always follow the Japanese model. They may recruit at various times during the year and do more hiring from the outside to fill middle- and upper-level management jobs. However, in general, a person who skips from job to job is still looked at with a critical eye and intense loyalty tends to keep people working for the same company for many, many years.

A NOTE ON USING INTERPRETERS

Although English is taught in schools, it is unrealistic to expect that all of your Japanese hosts and contacts will speak English. Younger Japanese who do speak English are not generally in positions of authority; older people in positions of authority usually do not speak English. Even if they have learned English, many Japanese are more comfortable reading or writing English than they are speaking English.

An interpreter can be one of your best resources in Japan. An interpreter who is either bicultural or is knowledgeable about the cultural differences between Japan and the U.S. can provide you not only with linguistic services but also with invaluable information about protocol, the nuances of Japanese culture, and the interpretation not only of words but also of nonverbal cues and hidden meanings.

Although it may seem easier to let your Japanese hosts provide an interpreter—after all, it will be one less thing on a very long list to worry about—you should carefully consider the possible impact of that option. Absolutely objective interpreters are hard to come by; the interpreter's loyalty is most likely to be toward his or her employer. Selecting your own interpreter ensures that your interests will be looked after. Even if your hosts are providing interpretive services, bringing your own interpreter can help verify the content of the exchange.

It is possible to locate an interpreter once you have arrived in Japan, but it is sometimes desirable to include your interpreter in the team coming from the U.S. Interpreters trained in Japan may not have had experience in the U.S. and would therefore be of limited cultural assistance.

Whenever possible, use an interpreter who is familiar with your industry and even with your company. If your company does not have access to a suitable individual and must hire someone unfamiliar to you or your company, arrange to meet with the interpreter before the meetings in order to brief him on your company, your goals, and your expectations. Provide the interpreter with as much documentation as possible to allow him or her to prepare for the meeting.

If you happen to have a Japanese-speaking team member and are relying on that person to interpret for the team, don't also expect him or her to enter into the negotiations. It not only becomes confusing, it is virtually impossible because interpreting requires a great deal of focus and concentration. So if any key member or members of your team speak Japanese, it is still wise to have an official interpreter who is not part of the actual negotiation.

If you are new to using interpreters, here are some guidelines.

- If each team has an interpreter present, each will translate the comments of his or her respective team. If only one is present, he will obviously be responsible for all translation.
- Always address the person to whom the comment or question is directed, not the interpreter. This takes practice, as most people tend to automatically turn to face the interpreter.
- Don't overwhelm the interpreter with words. You should pause for interpretation after every two or three sentences.

- Try to keep your sentences as uncomplicated as possible. A long, rambling sentence is very difficult to translate.
- Keep your vocabulary as simple as the situation will allow. Hopefully you will have taken the time beforehand to ensure that the interpreter has a vocabulary compatible with your needs, and you will have gone over any technical details with him or her.
- Avoid slang and colloquialisms. They may not be understood or, potentially even more disastrous, misunderstood if they are interpreted literally.
- The interpreter is not a machine. Interpreting takes an enormous amount of mental energy and is very draining. Allow at least a brief rest period after every hour or so. This is another argument in favor of having separate interpreters.
- If you are having trouble making yourself understood—and this goes for direct communication as well as interpreter-assisted communication—do not under any circumstance repeat your question or comment in ever-increasing volumes. The problem is comprehension, not hearing. Rephrase the statement until you reach understanding.

EIGHT

LAST NOTES

Hopefully this book has given you some insight into Japan and has given you some ways to prepare yourself for a successful, rewarding experience while living and working in Japan. The practical tips contained in this book should help you feel more comfortable as your journey begins, and the information on the Japanese culture will help you navigate as your journey continues.

In addition to the specific information covered in these seven chapters, don't forget these important guidelines for cross-cultural interaction anywhere around the globe:

• Learn about the culture you are visiting. The better you understand their culture the more prepared you will be to tune your skills to their frequency.

- Keep your sense of humor. Things are guaranteed to go wrong now and again and you will make mistakes. Your best defense is your ability to find humor in the situation.
- And finally, respect other cultures. Just because it's not the way you do things doesn't mean it's wrong.

Good luck in the exciting new environment that awaits you in Japan!

NINE

LANGUAGE NOTES

You don't necessarily need to be fluent in Japanese to get by while staying there for a short time while on business, but taking charge of a few key phrases in the language can aid you and your family in just getting by. The following supplement will familiarize you with the sounds of the Japanese language, allow you to get a hotel room, get around town, order a drink at the end of the day, and get help in case of an emergency. Additionally, we offer you some business terms and idiomatic expressions that may come up during a business meeting or encounter.

THE JAPANESE LANGUAGE

There are several things you should know and remember to make your understanding of Japanese easier:

1. Japanese syllables can be classified into five kinds:
   a. a vowel by itself
   b. a consonant by itself
   c. a consonant + a vowel
   d. a semi-vowel + a vowel
   e. a consonant + y + a vowel

2. In Japanese, verbs, adjectives, copulas (linking words), and certain endings are inflected in a number of categories.

3. Japanese has many so-called "particles." They are used very frequently to show the grammatical relationship within a sentence of one word to another. Mastery of these particles is a key to the rapid learning of Japanese.

4. Punctuation is used in Japanese as it is in English. The use of punctuation marks in the Japanese writing system is relatively new, and rules governing punctuation usage have not yet been firmly established.

5. The word order of Japanese sentences differs from the word order of English sentences. In Japanese, verbs come at the end of a sentence, rather than following the subject and preceding the object as they do in English.

6. Japanese has a complex system of "honorifics," words that reflect the relationship between the speakers and those about whom they are speaking. Different words and word forms are used to indicate the degrees of politeness. This concept is similar to the French differentiation between the formal "*vous*" and the informal "*tu*," but in Japanese there are more than a dozen ways to say "you." This supplement uses the most standard forms of the language, so that, unless otherwise indicated, each phrase can be said by both men and women in most situations, without sounding too casual or too formal.

THE SOUNDS OF
THE JAPANESE LANGUAGE

Many Japanese sounds are like sounds in English. Listen and repeat the following Japanese first names and notice which sounds are similar and which are different:

Akira	Jun
Aiko	Kiyoshi
Atsuko	Kuniko
Chieko	Makoto
Emiko	Mariko
Eijirō	Noboru
Fusao	Nobuko
Fusako	Osamu
Gantarō	Rentarō
Gīchi	Ryūichi
Haruo	Shinzō
Hideko	Susumu
Isō	Takashi
Itoko	Teruko
Jirō	Umeko

NOTE

- Each sound is pronounced clearly and crisply; sounds are not slurred over as they often are in English.
- Each syllable is spoken evenly for almost an equal length of time.
- Some names or words have an accented syllable, and some don't.

PHRASES

Listen to the phrase and repeat what you hear in the pause provided.

COMMON GREETINGS

Hello/Good morning.	Kon'nichiwa/ Ohayō gozaimasu.
Good evening.	Konbanwa.
Good-bye.	Sayōnara.
Polite form of address	last name + san
How are you? (informal)	Genki?
Fine, thanks. And you? (informal)	Ē, genki desu. Genki?
How are you? (formal)	Ogenki desu ka?
Fine, thanks. And you? (formal)	Hai, okagesamade. Ogenki desu ka?
What is your name?	Onamae wa?
My name is . . .	Watashi no namae wa . . .
Nice to meet you.	Hajimemashite.
I'll see you later.	Jā, mata.

POLITE EXPRESSIONS

Please.	Onegai shimasu.
Thank you.	Dōmo arigatō.
Thank you very much.	Dōmo arigatō gozaimasu.
You're welcome.	Dōitashimashite.
Yes, thank you.	Hai, dōmo arigatō.
No, thank you.	Īe, kekkō desu.
I beg your pardon.	Sumimasen, mō ichido onegai shimasu.
I'm sorry.	Sumimasen.
Pardon me. (informal)	Gomen'nasai.
Pardon me. (formal)	Sumimasen.
That's okay.	Ī desuyo.
It doesn't matter.	Daijōbu desu.
Do you speak English?	Eigo o hanashimasu ka?
Yes.	Hai.
No.	Īe.
Maybe.	Tabun.
I can speak a little.	Sukoshi hanashimasu.
I understand a little.	Sukoshi wakarimasu.
I don't understand.	Wakarimasen.

I don't speak Japanese very well.	Amari nihongo ga hanasemasen.
Would you repeat that, please?	Mō ichido onegaishimasu?
I don't know.	Wakarimasen.
No problem.	Daijōbu desu.
It's my pleasure.	Dō itashimashite.

NEEDS AND QUESTION WORDS

I'd like	. . . ga ī desu.
I need . . .	. . . ga hoshī desu.
What would you like?	Nani ga ī desu ka?
Please bring me . . .	. . . o motte kite kudasai.
I'm looking for . . .	. . . o sagashiteimasu.
I'm hungry.	Onaka ga sukimashita.
I'm thirsty	Nodo ga kawakimashita.
It's important.	Jūyō desu.
It's urgent.	Kyūyō desu.

How?	Dō desu ka?
How much?	Ikura desu ka?
How many?	Ikutsu desu ka?
Which?	Dore desu ka?
What?	Nan desu ka?
What kind of?	Don'na no desu ka?
Who?	Dare desu ka?
Where?	Doko desu ka?
When?	Itsu desu ka?
What does this mean?	Kore wa dō iu imi desu ka?
What does that mean?	Are wa dō iu imi desu ka?
How do you say . . . in Japanese?	. . . wa nihongo de nan to īmasu ka?

AT THE AIRPORT

Where is . . .	. . . wa doko desu ka?
customs?	Zeikan
passport control?	Ryoken shinsa (Pasupoto kontororu)

the information booth?	An'naisho
the ticketing counter?	Chiketto kauntā
baggage claim?	Tenimotsu hikitori (Baggeji kureimu)
the taxi stand?	Takushī noriba
the car rental?	Rentaru kā
the subway?	Chikatetsu
the bus stop?	Basu noriba

Is there a bus service to the city?	Machi made no basu ga arimasu ka?

Where are . . .	. . . wa doko desu ka?
the international departures?	Kokusaisen shuppatsu robī
the international arrivals?	Kokusaisen tōchaku robī

Where are you from?	Goshusshin wa dochira desu ka?
I am American.	Watashi wa amerika jin desu.
I am Canadian.	Watashi wa kanada jin desu.
I am British.	Watashi wa igirisu jin desu.
I am Australian.	Watashi wa ōsutoraria jin desu.

AT THE HOTEL, RESERVING A ROOM

I would like a room.	Heya no yoyaku o onegaishimasu.
for one person	Hitori beya
for two people	Futari beya
for tonight	Kon'ban
for two nights	Nihaku
for a week	Isshukan
Do you have a different room?	Betsuno haya ga arimasu ka?
with a bath	Ofuro tsuki
with a shower	Shawā tsuki
with a toilet	Toire tsuki
with air-conditioning	Eakon tsuki
How much is it?	Ikura desu ka?
I'd like to have my bill, please.	Seikyūsho o onegaishimasu.

Where can we find a good restaurant? Ī resutoran wa doko ni arimasu ka?

We'd like a(n) . . . restaurant. . . . resutoran ga ī n desu ga.

casual	Kajuaru na
elegant	Ereganto na
fast-food	Fāsuto fūdo no
inexpensive	Yasui
seafood	Shīfūdo no
vegetarian	Bejitarian no

Café Kissaten

Waiter! Waitress! Sumimasen! (excuse me)

A table for two, please. Futari de onegaishimasu.

I'd like a menu, please. Menyū o onegaishimasu.

I'd like to see the wine list, please. Wain risuto o onegaishimasu.

Appetizers Zensai

Main course Shusai (mein kosu)

Dessert Dezāto

What would you like? Nani ni nasaimasu ka?

What would you like to drink? (O)nomimono wa nani ni nasaimasu ka?

Can you recommend a good wine? Ii wain ga arimasu ka?

Wine, please. Wain o onegaishimasu.

Beer, please. Bīru o onegaishimasu.

I didn't order this. Kore wa chūmon shiteimasen.

That's all, thanks. Sore de zenbe desu.

The check, please. Okanjō (chekku) o onegaishimasu.

Cheers! To your health! Kanpai!

Where are the restrooms? Toire wa doko desu ka?

OUT ON THE TOWN

Where can I find . . . . . . wa doko desu ka?

an art museum?	Bijutsukan
a science museum?	Kagaku hakubutsukan

a history museum?	Rekishi hakubutsukan
a gallery?	Gyararī
interesting architecture?	Omoshiroi kenchikubutsu
a church?	Kyōkai
the zoo?	Dōbutsuen

I'd like . . .

to see a play.	Geki ga mitai desu.
to see a movie.	Eiga ga mitai desu.
to go to a concert.	Konsāto ni ikitai desu.
to go to the opera.	Opera ni ikitai desu.
to go sightseeing.	Kankō ga shitai desu.
to go on a bike ride.	Jitensha ni noritai desu.

SHOPPING

Where is the best place to go shopping for . . .	. . . o kaitai n desu ga, doko ga ichiban ī desu ka?
clothes?	Yōfuku
food?	Tabemono
souvenirs?	Omiyage
furniture?	Kagu
fabric?	Nuno
antiques?	Antīku
books?	Hon
sporting goods?	Supōtsu yōhin
electronics?	Denki seihin
computers?	Konpyūtā

DIRECTIONS

Excuse me.	Sumimasen.
Where is . . .	. . . wa doko desu ka?
the bus stop?	Basu tei
the subway station?	Chikatetsu no eki
the rest room?	Otearai
the taxi stand?	Takushī noriba
the nearest bank?	Chikaku no ginkō
the . . . hotel?	. . . hoteru
To the right	Migi ni itte kudasai.
To the left	Hidari ni itte kudasai.
Straight ahead	Massugu itte kudasai.
It's near here.	Kono chikaku desu.
Go back.	Modotte kudasai.
Next to	. . . no tonari desu.

Ordinal

0	Zero/rei	19	Jū kyū/Jū ku
1	Ichi	20	Ni jū
2	Ni	21	Ni jū ichi
3	San	22	Ni jū ni
4	Yon/shi	23	Ni jū san
5	Go	30	San jū
6	Roku	40	Yon jū
7	Nana/shichi	50	Go jū
8	Hachi	60	Roku jū
9	Kyū/ku	70	Nana jū
10	Jū	80	Hachi jū
11	Jū ichi	90	Kyu jū
12	Jū ni	100	Hyaku
13	Jū san	1,000	Sen
14	Jū yon/Jū shi	1,100	Sen hyaku
15	Jū go	2,000	Ni sen
16	Jū roku	10,000	Ichi man
17	Jū nana/Jū shichi	100,000	Jū man
18	Jū hachi	1,000,000	Hyaku man

Cardinal

first	Ichi ban	eleventh	Jū ichi ban
second	Ni ban	twelfth	Jū ni ban
third	San ban	thirteenth	Jū san ban
fourth	Yon ban	fourteenth	Jū yon ban
fifth	Go ban	fifteenth	Jū go ban
sixth	Roku ban	sixteenth	Jū roku ban
seventh	Nana ban	seventeenth	Jū nana ban
eighth	Hachi ban	eighteenth	Jū hachi ban
ninth	Kyu ban	nineteenth	Jū kyū ban
tenth	Jū ban	twentieth	Ni jū ban

twenty-first	Ni jū ichi ban	seventieth	Nana jū ban
twenty-second	Ni jū ni ban	eightieth	Hachi jū ban
thirtieth	San jū ban	ninetieth	Kyu jū ban
fortieth	Yon jū ban	hundredth	Hyaku ban
fiftieth	Go jū ban	thousandth	Sen ban
sixtieth	Roku jū ban		

TIME

What time is it?	Ima wa nan ji desu ka?
It is noon.	Shōgo desu.
It is midnight.	Mayonaka desu.
It is 9:00 am.	Gozen ku ji desu.
It is 1:00 pm.	Gogo ichi ji desu.
It is 3 o'clock.	San ji desu.
It's 5:15.	Goji jūgo fun desu.
It's 7:30.	Shichi ji han desu.
It's 9:45.	Ku ji yon jū go fun desu.
Now	Ima
Later	Ato(de)
Immediately	Shikyū
Soon	Sugu

DAYS OF THE WEEK/ MONTHS OF THE YEAR

Monday	Getsu yōbi
Tuesday	Ka yōbi
Wednesday	Sui yōbi
Thursday	Moku yōbi
Friday	Kin yōbi
Saturday	Do yōbi
Sunday	Nichi yōbi
What day is today?	Kyō wa nan yōbi desu ka?

January	Ichi gatsu
February	Ni gatsu
March	San gatsu
April	Shi gatsu
May	Go gatsu
June	Roku gatsu
July	Shichi gatsu
August	Hachi gatsu
September	Ku gatsu
October	Jū gatsu
November	Jū ichi gatsu
December	Jū ni gatsu

What is the date today?	Kyō wa nan nichi desu ka?
Today is Thursday, September 22nd.	Kyō wa ku gatsu ni jū ni nichi, moku yōbi desu.
Yesterday was Wednesday, September 21st.	Kinō wa kugatsu ni jū ichi nichi, sui yōbi deshita.
Tomorrow is Friday, September 23rd.	Ashita wa ku gatsu ni jū san nichi, kin yōbi desu.

MODERN CONNECTIONS

Where can I find . . .	. . . wa doko desu ka?
a telephone?	Denwa
a fax machine?	Fakkusu
an Internet connection?	Intānetto
How do I call the United States?	Amerika ni denwa o kaketai n desu ga?

I need . . .	
a fax sent.	Fakkusu o okuritai n desu ga.
a hook-up to the Internet.	Intānetto ni setsuzokushitai n desu ga.
a computer.	Konpyūtā o tsukaitai n desu ga.
a package sent overnight.	Kozutsumi o sokutatsu de okuritai n desu ga.
some copies made.	Kopī o toritai n desu ga.

| a VCR and monitor. | Bideo to terebi o tsukaitai n desu ga. |
| an overhead projector and markers. | OHP to mākā o tsukaitai n desu ga. |

EMERGENCIES AND SAFETY

Help!	Tasukete (kudasai)!
Fire!	Kaji (desu)!
I need a doctor.	Isha o yonde kudasai.
Call an ambulance!	Kyūkyūsha o yonde kudasai!
What happened?	Dō shimashita ka?
My wife is/My husband is/My friend is/Someone is . . .	(Tsuma ga . . . /Shujin ga . . . /Tomodachi ga . . . /Dareka ga . . .)
I am very sick.	Byōki desu.
My husband is having a heart attack.	Shujin ga shinzō hossa o okoshiteimasu.
My wife is choking.	Tsuma ga chissoku shiteimasu.
My friend is losing consciousness.	Tomodachi ga ishiki o ushinatteimasu.
I am about to vomit.	Hakike ga shimasu.
Someone is having a seizure.	Dareka ga hossa o okoshiteimasu.
I am stuck.	Hasamatte shimaimashita.
I can't breathe.	Iki ga dekimasen.
I tripped and fell.	Tsumazuite korobimashita.
I cut myself.	Kitte shimaimashita.
I drank too much.	Nomisugimashita.
I don't know.	Wakarimasen.
I've injured my . . .	. . . ni kega o shimashita.
head.	Atama
neck.	Kubi
back.	Senaka
arm.	Ude
leg.	Ashi
foot.	Ashi
eye.	Me
I've been robbed.	Dorobō ni aimashita.

accept (to)	Ukeireru
account(s)	Akaunto
agenda(s)	Gidai
asset(s)	Zaisan
benefit(s)	Rieki
black market	Yami ichi
boss	Jōshi
buy (to)	Kau
capital	Shihon
close a deal (to)	Torihiki o oeru
cold call(s)	Nukiuchi denwa
colleague(s)	Dōryō
contract(s)	Keiyaku
copyright (©)	Chosakuken
deal(s)	Torihiki
economy	Keizai
embargo(es)	Kinshi
employee(s)	Jūgyōin
employer(s)	Koyōsha
global village	Gurōbaru birejji
gross domestic product (GDP)	Kokunai sōseisan
gross national product (GNP)	Kokumin sōseisan
guarantee(s)	Hoshō
human resources (HR)	Jinji
income	Shūnyū
information technology (IT)	IT (ai ti)
interview	Mensetsu
issue(s)	Mondai
item(s)	Kōmoku
job(s)	Shigoto
junior executive	Buka
labor (labor force)	Rōdō
liquidate (to)	Seisai suru
meeting(s)	Kaigi
negotiate (to)	Kōshō
offer(s)	Mōshide/teian

option(s)	Sentaku
presentation(s)	Teishutsu/teian
price(s)	Kakaku
product(s)	Shōhin
profit(s)	Rieki
propose (to)	Teian suru
quality	Shitsu
quantity	Ryō
reject (to)	Kotowaru
résumé	Rirekisho
sell (to)	Uru
seminar(s)	Seminā/Zeminaru
senior executive	Jōshi
service(s)	Gyōmu
specification(s)	Meisai
stock(s)	Kabu
supervisor(s)	Kantoku
trademark (™)	Shōhyō/tore–do māku
training session(s)	Kunren kikan
union(s)	Rōdō kumiai
yield	Mikaeri

COMPUTER TERMINOLOGY

Computers are a part of business all over the world, and every day more companies and individuals come to rely on the computer. As the technology grows, the terminology broadens with it to include a multitude of phrases. Following are several terms that are used frequently when dealing with computers in the workplace.

access privileges	Akusesu token
application	Aparikashun
attachment	Tempu
browser	Burauzā
cc	Cc (shī shī)
crash	Kurashu
cyberspace	Saibāsupe–su
database	Dēta bēsu

dot-com	Dotto komu
double-click	Daburu kurikku
download	Daunrōdo
file	Fairu
hard copy	Hādo kopi
hard drive	Hādo doraibu
hardware	Hādo weā
HTML (Hypertext Mark-up Language)	HTML (eichi ti emu eru)
ISP (Internet Service Provider)	Intāneto purobaidā
laptop	Nōtobukku
log on	Rogu on
log off	Rogu ofu
Mac or Macintosh	Makku
mailing list	Meiru risuto
mainframe	Furēmu
modem	Modemu
multimedia	Maruchimedia
network	Nettowāku
online	Onrain
password	Pasuwādo
PC (personal computer)	Pasokon
reboot	Tachiageru
scroll	Sukurōru
search engine	Sāchi enjin
search the Internet	Intānetto o kensaku suru
server	Sābā
software	Sofutoweā
technical support	Sapōto
URL (Uniform Resource Locator)	URL (yū āru eru)
user-friendly	Yūzā furendorī
Web site	Webu saito

BUSINESS IDIOMATIC EXPRESSIONS

Let's get the ball rolling.
Sa, hajimemashō.
We're making a lot of headway.
Junchō desu.

Think outside the box.

>Motto hiroi shiya o motte kudasai.

Run it up the flagpole.

>Minna ni shirasemasho.

>(lit: Let everyone know about it.)

I'm between a rock and a hard place.

>Ikizumatte dōshiyo mo nai.

>(lit: I'm in a bad situation with no foreseeable good ending.)

I'd like everyone to get on board.

>Icchi danketsu shimashō.

>(lit: I'd like everyone to participate and pledge his or her support to the situation.)

I'm playing devil's advocate.

>Igi o moshiagemasu.

>(lit: I'm presenting the opposing argument to the situation.)

Keep me in the loop.

>Renraku shite kudasai.

>(lit: Keep me informed about the situation.)

They're dragging their heels on this one.

>Karera wa gakkari shiteimasu.

>(lit: They're being reluctant and slow to act.)

We'll touch base.

>Renraku o toriaimashō.

>(lit: We'll keep in touch regarding the situation.)

He's given me the green light.

>OK ga demashita.

>(lit: He's told me it's okay to start work on that.)

I need these reports yesterday.

>Daishikyu onegaishimasu.

He's just a flash in the pan.

>Kare wa mikkabōzu da.

>(lit: He's a person with short-lived accomplishments.)

Put your nose to the grindstone.

>Shigoto ni torikakarimashō.

>(lit: Get to work.)

Get your foot in the door.

Saisho no shigoto o totte kitte kudasai.

(lit: Get a first appointment./Get inside the company.)

It's a Catch-22.

Mō dō nimonaranai.

(lit: It's a situation where you can't win.)

The company has gone belly-up.

Kaisha wa tōsan shiteshimaimashita.

(lit: The company has gone bankrupt.)

Just bite the bullet.

Sono koto ni wa me o tsubutte kudasai. (Pretend not to see the situation.)

Gaman shite kudasai. (Just be patient.)

(lit: Just accept the unpleasant situation.)

The company is cleaning house.

Kaisha wa takusan no hito o kubi ni shiteimasu.

(lit: The company is firing a lot of employees.)

We need to put our heads together.

Icchidanketsu shite kangae mashō.

(lit: We need to think together.)

He's got a lot of clout.

Kare wa eikyōryoku ga aru.

(lit: He has a lot of significant influence.)

Is the glass half full or half empty?

Sansei desu ka, hantai desu ka?

(lit: Do you have a positive or negative perception of the situation?)

That's a kick in the pants.

Sore wa gakkari desu ne.

(lit: That's discouraging.)

There's a light at the end of the tunnel.

Mada nozomi wa arimasu.

(lit: There's still hope.)

It's a dog-eat-dog world.

Jakuniku kyōshoku no sekai.

(lit: It's a competitive world.)

We're making inroads.

> Junchō desu.
>
> (lit: We're making progress.)

The project is dead in the water.

> Kono purojekuto wa ikizumatteiru.
>
> (lit: The project is not going anywhere.)

Let's go back to the drawing board.

> Atama kara yarinao shimashō.
>
> (lit: Let's start over.)

Let's lay our cards on the table.

> Tenouchi o akasō.
>
> (lit: Let's show our plans openly.)

Don't burn your bridges.

> Atomodori dekinai yō na koto wa shinaide
> kudasai.
>
> (lit: Don't make a situation where you can't
> go back and change things.)

Keep on your toes.

> Kakugo shite kudasai.
>
> (lit: Be ready.)

Let's not reinvent the wheel.

> Kokomade kite saishokara yarinaosu no wa
> yamemashō.
>
> (lit: Let's not start from scratch for something
> for which the work has already been done.)

She's sitting on the fence.

> Kanojo wa kesshin ga tsukanai de iru.
>
> (lit: She's refusing to make a decision.)

When push comes to shove . . .

> Dōshitemo to iunara . . .

She's got plenty on her plate.

> Shigoto ga yamazumi desu.
>
> (lit: She has a lot of work to do.)

I can't make heads or tails of this.

> Sappari wakarimasen.

It's Greek to me.
    Chin pun kan pun desu.
That's just a ballpark figure.
    Donburi kanjō.
We need to strike while the iron is hot.
    Kugi wa atsui uchi ni ute.

BEFORE YOU GO

Passports. Be sure that each member of your family has one, and that each is valid for the length of your assignment. Children should have separate passports; otherwise they will not be allowed to travel alone or with an adult other than their parents, even in an emergency.

Visas. Check with the embassy of any countries you will be in for necessary visas. Requirements vary by country, especially for international relocation. As you travel, don't overlook the fact that some countries require a transit visa for people passing through the country, even if you don't get off your plane or train.

Vaccinations/inoculations. Check for recommended vaccinations or inoculations for the country you will be living in, as well as any countries you intend to visit. (This is listed on the U.S. Department of State Consular Information Sheet; see item 13 below.) The Department of Health and Human Services' Office of Public Health Services is able to issue an International Certificate of Vaccination containing your personal history of vaccinations. The ICV is approved by the World Health Organization.

Insurance. Make sure that your insurance will cover you while you are abroad. Check now, before you need it. If it won't, do some research to find out how to supplement or change your insurance so that you are adequately covered.

International driver's permits. Although you can use your U.S. or Canadian driver's license in some countries, it is generally advisable to obtain an international driver's permit. This is available from AAA for a small fee and does not require taking a test. International driver's permits are valid for one year; after that time, you may have to get a local driver's license. Be sure that you get a permit that is valid for the country(ies) that you will be driving in.

Pets. Check with the consulate of your host country to find out about restrictions and requirements for bringing pets into the country. Most countries require a health and immunization certificate from a veterinarian; some have quarantine periods upon arrival.

Medical records. Obtain complete medical records for each member of your family. Have one copy on hand for the trip in case of an emergency.

Prescriptions and medication. If you or anyone in your family takes prescription medication, especially those containing narcotics, have your doctor give you a letter stating what the drug is and why it is necessary. Be sure you get a list of the Latin names of all prescription drugs from your doctor, since brand names vary from country to country. Take a six-month supply of any prescription medication, if possible. All medication, prescription or over-the-counter, should be in its original bottle and clearly labeled. Drug and narcotics laws are very strict in many countries, and you do not want to run afoul of them. Ask your dentist if it is advisable to have fluoride treatments, especially for children; most countries do not add fluoride to the water as the U.S. does.

School records. If you have chosen a school for your child, you will probably have already made arrangements to forward your child's records. If not, be sure to request a complete set of records to take with you for each child. Don't forget school records, including diplomas and certificates, for yourself or your partner if either one of you might take continuing education classes while you're abroad!

Wills and guardianship documents. Your personal affairs should be in order before you leave. Your lawyer or a family member should have access to these documents in the case of an emergency.

Power of attorney. Assign power of attorney to act in your interest at home, if necessary. (A power of attorney does not have to be permanent and can be nullified when you return, if desired.)

Paying bills. If you've got a mortgage or other payments that must be paid while you're abroad, decide how to handle them before you go. There are several options, including maintaining a checking account at home and paying bills yourself, arranging for your bank to pay them (not all banks offer this service), or having your lawyer, accountant, or a family member pay them.

Travel advisories. The U.S. Department of State publishes a 1- to 2-page consular information sheet on each country that covers basic topics such as medical and safety information, as well as addresses and phone numbers of U.S. consulates in the country. When necessary, travel advisories are released regarding areas of political instability, terrorist activity, etc. Check before you travel. (Consular information sheets and travel advisories are also available on many online services, such as CompuServe, and at the State Department Web site at http://www.state.gov.)

Copies of important documents. Make two copies of important documents; take one with you and leave one with your lawyer or a family member. Important documents include:

- Passport (the inside front cover, which contains your passport number and other information)
- Visas, transit visas, and tourist cards
- Driver's license, international driving permit
- Insurance card and other information
- International Certificate of Vaccination, medical records

Special needs. If you or anyone in your family has any special needs, check that appropriate facilities and services are available from hotels and airlines. Not all are equipped to deal with infants, persons with physical disabilities, and other concerns, such as medication that requires special handling or refrigeration.

Change of address. Be sure to inform all of the necessary people and companies of your change of address. Some companies will assess a service fee for mailing bills and statements internationally. Write to each company, and keep a copy of the notice in case a problem develops and to remind you what bills and statements you should be receiving. Don't forget the following:

- Banks where you are keeping local accounts or have loans
- Credit cards, including department store and gasoline cards
- Stockbroker or stock transfer agent, retirement account agents
- Lawyer
- Accountant
- Insurance company, including homeowners, personal, medical, and life
- Tax offices in any city or state where you have property tax liabilities
- Voter registration office
- Magazines and periodicals
- Alumni associations and professional memberships

Bank letter of reference. It is often difficult to establish banking services in a country where you have no credit history. It will help to have your bank or credit card write you a letter of good credit. Also helpful is a letter from your local office in your new country that states your salary. Some banks now have branches in many countries; you may be able to open an expatriate account at home before you go that will allow you access to bank services worldwide.

Close unnecessary accounts. However, you should leave open one or two key accounts that will provide you with a credit history when you return. Also make arrangements to terminate telephone, utility, garbage collection, newspaper delivery, and other services as necessary.

Inventory. An inventory of all of your belongings is helpful for shipping and insurance purposes. Enlist the help of an appraiser as necessary for items of value.

Packing. Put a card with your name and address inside each piece of luggage and each box being shipped. Don't put your passport in the boxes to be shipped!

CONTACTS AND RESOURCES

BUSINESS AND INFORMATION RESOURCES

Embassy of Japan

2520 Massachusetts Avenue NW
Washington D.C. 20008
Tel: (202) 238–6700
Fax: (202) 328–2187
www.us.emb-japan.go.jp

Consulate General of Japan

Following is a partial list of Japanese consulates in major U.S. cities. For information on other consulates, you can call one of the consulates listed or search the Internet.

299 Park Avenue
New York, NY 10171
Tel: (212) 371-8222
www.cgj.org

Olympia Centre #1100
737 North Michigan Avenue
Chicago, IL 60611
Tel: (312) 280-0400
Fax: (312) 280-9568
www.chicago.us.emb-japan.go.jp

One Alliance Center
Suite 1600
3500 Lenox Road
Atlanta, GA 30326
Tel: (404) 240-4300
Fax: (404) 240-4311
www.atlanta.us.emb-japan.go.jp

350 South Grand Avenue, Suite 1700
Los Angeles, CA 90071
Tel: (213) 617-6700
www.la.us.emb-japan.go.jp

American Embassy Tokyo

1-10-5 Akasaka
Minato-ku, Tokyo 107-8420
General telephone: (03) 3224-5000
Visa inquiries: 0990-526-160
Passport inquiries: (03) 3224-5168
Fax: (03) 3505-1862

U.S. Mailing Address

APO AP 96337-5004
USA

In addition to the U.S. embassy in Beijing, there are U.S. Consulates General in Fukuoka, Naha (Okinawa), Osaka, and Sapporo.

Japan External Trade Organization (JETRO)

www.jetro.org

JETRO is a Japanese government-supported organization that promotes mutually beneficial trade and investment relations between Japan and other nations. JETRO has more than 100 offices worldwide including eight locations in the U.S.

American Chamber of Commerce in Japan

www.accj.or.jp

The ACCJ promotes commerce between the U.S. and Japan, supports measures to benefit and protect the interests of U.S. companies, and presents a variety of programs that keep chamber members abreast of current business practices and trends.

Japan Society

www.japansociety.org

The Japan Society is an American institution with individual and corporate members that promotes understanding and enlightened relations between the U.S. and Japan.

Japan Information Network

www.jinjapan.org

SOCIAL AND EXPATRIATE RESOURCES

Please note that in addition to the organizations listed, many of the Web-based resources listed in this section offer information and support via an online community; you can find more information with a click of the mouse when you visit their Web sites.

Tokyo American Club

www.tac-club.org

The Tokyo American Club is a private membership club offering activities and support to the international community in Japan. Note: You do not have to be an American to join the Tokyo American Club.

Kaisha Society

www.kaisha.gol.com/index.html

The Kaisha Society in Tokyo offers a forum for global professionals in Tokyo to learn, communicate, and grow.

Association of Foreign Wives of Japanese (AFWJ)

home.att.ne.jp/surf/cei/AFWJ.html

The AFWJ provides friendship, support, mutual help in adapting to Japanese society, and opportunities for social, emotional, educational, and professional growth to women "of any national or cultural origin, other than Japanese born and raised in Japan, who is engaged to, is, or has been married to a man of Japanese national or cultural origin."

RESOURCES FOR MOVING ABROAD

Video Overseas, Inc.

246 8th Avenue
2nd Floor
New York, NY 10011
Tel: (212) 645-0797 or (800) 317-6945
Fax: (212) 242-8144
www.videooverseas.com

Video Overseas, Inc. offers household appliances and electronics that are adapted or manufactured for international use.

Air Animal, Inc. (U.S. and Canada)

Tel: (800) 635-3448
www.airanimal.com
Air Animal, Inc. provides information and assistance on moving
your pet abroad.

HELPFUL WEB SITES

Escape Artist

www.escapeartist.com

Expat Exchange

www.expatexchange.com

Utopia

www.utopia-asia.com
Asian gay and lesbian resources

TRAVEL IN JAPAN

Japanese Automobile Federation (JAF)

Tel: 03-3436-2811
www.jaf.or.jp/e/index_e.htm
JAF is the Japanese equivalent of the American/Canadian Automobile Associations (AAA and CAA). JAF has regional offices all over
Japan; contact information can be found on their web page.

U.S. Centers for Disease Control and Prevention

Atlanta, Georgia

Tel: (877) FYI-TRIP [(877) 394-8747]

www.cdc.gov/travel/index.htm

The U.S. Centers for Disease Control and Prevention provide health advisories, immunization recommendations or requirements, and advice on food and drinking-water safety for regions and countries.

CROSS-CULTURAL RESOURCES

Terra Cognita

www.terracognita.com

Terra Cognita offers videos, books, audio, and Internet training and resources for living and working in Japan and around the world.

METRIC CONVERSIONS

Although a sizing conversion chart can be a step in the right direction, an accurate fit is found only by trying the item on, just as you would at home. Most Westerners find that they cannot wear off-the-rack clothes purchased in Japan, as the Japanese frame is simply smaller than a Western one. Some clothing has metric sizing, the conversions for which follow, although they are merely guidelines.

WOMEN'S DRESSES AND SKIRTS

U.S.	4	6	8	10	12	14	16	18			
Japan	3	5	7	9	11	13	15	17			
British	6	8	10	12	14	16	18	20			
Metric	34	36	38	40	42	44	46	48			

WOMEN'S BLOUSES AND SWEATERS

U.S.	4	6	8	10	12	14	16	18	20	22	24
Japan	3	5	7	9	11	13	15				
British	26	28	30	32	34	36	38	40	42	44	46
Metric	32	34	36	38	40	42	44	46	48	50	52

WOMEN'S SHOES

U.S.	5	6	7	8	9	10
Japan	22	23	24	25	26	27
British	3½	4½	5½	6½	7½	8½
Metric	37	38	39	40	41	42

MEN'S SUITS

U.S.	34	36	38	40	42	44	46	48
Japan	S	—	M	L	—	XL	—	—
British	34	36	38	40	42	44	46	48
Metric	44	46	48	50	52	54	56	58

MEN'S SHIRTS

U.S.	14½	15	15½	16	16½	17	17½	18
Japan	37	38	39	41	42	43	44	45
British	14½	15	15½	16	16½	17	17½	18
Metric	37	38	39	41	42	43	44	45

MEN'S SHOES

U.S.	7	8	9	10	11	12	13
Japan	26	27	28	29	30	31	32
British	6½	7½	8½	9½	10½	11½	12½
Metric	39	40	41	42	43	44	45

CHILDREN'S CLOTHING

U.S.	3	4	5	6	6x
British	18	20	22	24	26
Metric	98	104	110	116	122

CHILDREN'S SHOES

U.S.	8	9	10	11	12	13	1	2	3
British	7	8	9	10	11	12	13	1	2
Metric	24	25	27	28	29	30	32	33	34

DISTANCE

1 yard	0.914 meters
1 foot	0.305 meters
1 inch	2.54 centimeters
1 mile	1.609 kilometers
1 meter	1.094 yards
1 meter	3.279 feet
1 centimeter	0.394 inches
1 kilometer	0.622 miles

SPEED

1 mph	1.609 kph
30 mph	48 kph
55 mph	88 kph
65 mph	105 kph
80 mph	128 kph
100 mph	160 kph
1 kph	0.622 mph
55 kph	34 mph
65 kph	40 mph
80 kph	50 mph
100 kph	62 mph
150 kph	93 mph

DRY MEASURES

1 pint	.551 liter
1 quart	1.101 liters
1 liter	0.908 dry quarts

LIQUID MEASURES

1 fluid ounce	29.57 milliliters
1 pint	0.47 liter
1 quart	0.946 liters
1 gallon	3.785 liters
1 liter	1.057 liquid quarts

WEIGHT

1 ounce	28.35 grams
1 pound	0.45 kilograms
1 gram	0.035 ounce
1 kilogram	2.20 pounds

TEMPERATURE

To convert Fahrenheit into Celsius, subtract 32, multiply by 5 and divide by 9.

To convert Celsius into Fahrenheit, multiply by 9, divide by 5, and add 32.

FAHRENHEIT	→ CELSIUS	CELSIUS	→ FAHRENHEIT
-20	-28	-50	-58
-15	-26	-45	-49
-10	-23	-40	-40
-5	-20	-35	-31
0	-17	-30	-22
5	-15	-25	-13
10	-12	-20	-4
15	-9	-15	5
20	-6	-10	14
25	-3	-5	23
30	-1	0	32
35	1	5	41

FAHRENHEIT	→ CELSIUS	CELSIUS	→ FAHRENHEIT
40	4	10	50
45	7	15	59
50	10	20	68
55	12	25	77
60	15	30	86
65	18	35	95
70	21	40	104
75	23	45	113
80	26	50	122
85	29	55	131
90	32	60	140
95	35	65	149
100	37	70	158
105	40	75	167
110	43	80	176
115	46	85	185
120	48	90	194
125	51	95	203
150	65	100	212
175	79	105	221
200	93	110	230
225	107	115	239
250	121	120	248
275	135	125	257
300	148	150	302
325	162	175	347
350	176	200	392
375	190	225	437
400	204	250	482
425	218	275	527
450	232	300	572
475	246		
500	260		